fresh PASSION®

GET A BRAND OR DIE A GENERIC®

MICHAEL D. BROWN

GREENLEAF
BOOK GROUP PRESS

This publication is designed to provide accurate and authoritative information in regard to the subject matter covered. It is sold with the understanding that the publisher and author are not engaged in rendering legal, accounting, or other professional services. If legal advice or other expert assistance is required, the services of a competent professional should be sought.

Published by Greenleaf Book Group Press
Austin, Texas
www.gbgpress.com

Copyright ©2013 Michael D. Brown

All rights reserved.

No part of this book may be reproduced, stored in a retrieval system, or transmitted by any means, electronic, mechanical, photocopying, recording, or otherwise, without written permission from the copyright holder.

Distributed by Greenleaf Book Group LLC

For ordering information or special discounts for bulk purchases, please contact Greenleaf Book Group LLC at PO Box 91869, Austin, TX 78709, 512.891.6100.

Design and composition by Greenleaf Book Group LLC
Cover design by Francisco Bennett, Made by ISO6

Publisher's Cataloging-In-Publication Data
(Prepared by The Donohue Group, Inc.)

Brown, Michael D., 1972-
    Fresh passion : get a brand or die a generic / by Michael D. Brown.—Professional ed., 1st ed.

    p. ; cm.

    Issued also as an ebook.
    Includes bibliographical references.
    ISBN: 978-1-60832-411-8

    1. Self-presentation. 2. Branding (Marketing) 3. Self-actualization (Psychology) I. Title. II. Title: Get a brand or die a generic

BF697.5.S44 B76 2013
155.24   2012944245

Part of the Tree Neutral® program, which offsets the number of trees consumed in the production and printing of this book by taking proactive steps, such as planting trees in direct proportion to the number of trees used: www.treeneutral.com

Printed in the United States of America on acid-free paper

12 13 14 15 16 17   10 9 8 7 6 5 4 3 2 1

First Edition

This Fresh book is dedicated to my mother, my ten brothers and sisters, and the hundreds of world-class professionals I have had the highest privilege of leading.

THANK YOU!

contents

PREFACE vii
ACKNOWLEDGMENTS xv
ABOUT THIS FRESH GREEN BOOK xix
1 GET A BRAND OR DIE A GENERIC 1
2 ACHIEVING FRESHNESS 17
3 *fresh* PASSION: PREPARING YOURSELF 39
4 *fresh* PASSION: ASPIRING TO REACH YOUR GOALS ... 61
5 *fresh* PASSION: STAYING LASER-FOCUSED 81
6 *fresh* PASSION: SELLING YOUR VALUE 101
7 *fresh* PASSION: INVIGORATING YOURSELF 131
8 *fresh* PASSION: OMITTING THE NEGATIVE 149
9 *fresh* PASSION: NAILING THE BRAND 169
   FINAL THOUGHTS: THE LAST BITE OF THE BROWNIE ... 209
   ABOUT MICHAEL D. BROWN 217
   ABOUT MICHAEL D. BROWN'S BRAND LOGO 221

preface

I have literally been building a brand geared toward achieving personal and professional success for almost my entire life. It all started in fourth grade back in Holmes County, Mississippi, when I took a job working as a handyman and housecleaner for a wealthy lady living on the "right" side of the tracks, who I will call Norma.

The task of providing customer service to Norma was by no means an easy one. Norma felt that her social position entitled her to be crotchety and demanding, as well as physically violent if her every whim was not fulfilled. I have to admit that at times she could be very accommodating, but this accommodating demeanor was usually part of some elaborate mind game she would play to keep me from getting too comfortable. And the harder I worked, the more she demanded. Every day I walked on eggshells.

The notion of "walking on eggshells" is the perfect lead-in to a story that I think exemplifies the challenges and obstacles posed by working for Norma. I was cooking breakfast one Saturday morning—by this point I was tall enough to reach the stove, so it wasn't a problem. Normally, she wanted her eggs "hard," but I never knew exactly how hard "hard" was supposed to be. It seemed like I never got it right. But on this particular Saturday, I thought I had it down pat. Imagine my surprise when she screamed, "You just don't get it! You should know by now!"

I carefully explained that the eggs were cooked the same way they had been the previous weekend, when she appeared to like them. Norma took this as license to raise her hand and shove me in the chest. "Don't talk back to me like that," she said. Prior to this incident, I had never talked back to her. And I wasn't even trying to "talk back" so much as I was merely attempting to understand why she was upset with the eggs when she had liked them the week before. After she pushed me, I walked away.

The next weekend, she led me to believe things were fine again. She was being accommodating, but I never knew how she would react to any given situation. And I don't think I ever did get the eggs right!

In a classic example of Norma's mind games, after the egg incident she eased up on her criticism of my cooking skills, but then she moved on to criticizing how I cleaned the glass and mirrors in her house. I always used too much or too little glass cleaner, and she never stopped finding something new to keep me on edge.

Norma knew I was a perfectionist who always sought to exceed expectations, and I think she thought, "I'll always tell him he's not doing it right, that way he'll work harder." To make matters worse, when I didn't respond the first time she shoved me, it became a license for her to push me around.

This unpleasant situation offered me two choices: Stick it out or leave.

As one of ten siblings being raised by my widowed mother, living in the fourth-poorest county in the country, leaving did not appear to be a viable option. Despite the many hardships, I enjoyed and needed this job's financial compensation. So I grinned and bore it for two whole years, swallowing all the pride a nine-year-old boy could have.

Many of you are probably shaking your head with a sad, wistful look on your face, feeling sorry for that poor little boy stuck between an awful boss and extreme poverty in rural Mississippi many years ago. Save your pity—instead you can celebrate that I experienced this unfortunate incident so early in life. Working for Norma is probably one of the best things that ever happened to me. How could that be possible? Glad you asked.

First, striving to please an impossible taskmaster taught me that to succeed in life, you must work your very hardest, stay focused on delivering superior results that exceed expectation, and always give 120 percent, even when deep down you know you will still be criticized. Ultimately, a good job speaks for itself, and if you consistently deliver superior results, your boss, critics, and other observers will be left with no choice but to recognize you as someone who can deliver, and you will become known as someone who produces superior results regardless of the circumstances. As painful as working for Norma often was, the experience toughened me and served as the foundation of my personal Michael D. Brown brand; a brand built on consistently delivering top-notch results, continually looking for ways to exceed expectations, always offering a fresh experience, and satisfying even the most demanding customers, bosses, and clients, all with a professional and pleasant personal demeanor.

Developing this brand was not an easy process or a quick one. Norma was the first unfair boss I worked for, but she was hardly the last. Later in my professional career, I found myself flipping burgers at a popular fast-food joint while I was getting my undergraduate degree in management at Jackson State University. Here I learned a very different lesson. I originally applied to fill an advertised cashier opening, but the general manager told me they really needed someone to work the grill. Even though I had previous cashier experience and great references, and *I was currently studying management at Jackson State University*, I still wasn't considered a viable candidate for the cashier position. So the managers hid me back in the kitchen.

Instead of complaining about this grueling and greasy job, I started planning my escape route. I wound up driving immense results through and with people, cutting wait time at the drive-through window from two minutes and thirty seconds to one minute and twenty seconds. It was teamwork "Michael D. Brown style," and the employees loved it. Yet despite my results and the love the whole staff had for me, it was many months before I finally got promoted to cashier.

Eventually, the general manager admitted to me that the regional manager had told him that he didn't want to see black people as cashiers at the front counter waiting on customers because the restaurant was located in an affluent area, and he didn't see having black people working at the front counter as being good for business.

Since then, I have always tried to overcompensate by delivering superior results and always exceeding expectations due to both obvious and camouflaged racism. As a result of this experience and others like it,

I couldn't escape the thought that I had to do much better than anyone else by keeping my skills fresh and being able to deliver competitive results. My intense focus on the front line, which generated results and output that beat expectations, helped me climb the corporate ladder because no one in the organizations, firms, or corporations I worked for could deny the results. I kept the attention off me personally (and my skin color) by delivering better than anyone else and building a professional "cushion" for myself.

These two early professional experiences had a tremendous impact on both my personal worldview and on how I conduct myself professionally—in short, my personal brand. I learned that by properly believing in myself, applying myself, and presenting myself, I could achieve tremendous personal and professional success, despite any obstacle. Childhood poverty, harsh and unyielding bosses, outright racial discrimination—none of these could prevent me from reaching my potential unless I allowed them to. By building a successful brand, I took control of my circumstances instead of letting my circumstances take control of me.

Having a successful personal brand is the difference between having a job and having a career. As the title of the book indicates, if you allow yourself to be "generic," that is, one more average working stiff with no obvious special, outstanding, and competitive qualities, you will not attract people and successful opportunities to you. You will be stuck in a succession of unrewarding and career-stagnating low-paying jobs that offer no real financial success or advancement opportunity. Financial success is different for everyone, and only you can define what it means—so I challenge you to identify what financial success is *for you*, and write it down so you have a goal. And while work is surely not everything, or even the most important thing, in life, if you are stuck in a professional rut, it is very difficult to lead a truly rewarding personal life.

This rut will begin to rob your mind, consume valuable focus time that could be used to achieve personal and professional success, and drain your personal happiness, and in many cases your self-worth, because you will spend a large part of your day and/or your life reminding yourself how bad things really are.

On the contrary, if you build a personal brand that offers competitive value and a fresh experience to companies, organizations, institutions, your clients and customers (especially if you are an entrepreneur), higher learning centers, etc., you will have the foundation needed to lead a successful professional career and a more fulfilling personal life, which will help you avoid an existence marred by personal and professional poverty.

While I was in college, I articulated my methodology for creating a successful personal brand (though at that time I hadn't classified it into this brilliant acronym). I call it Fresh PASSION, a convenient acronym that stands for:

PREPARING **Y**OURSELF
ASPIRING TO **R**EACH **Y**OUR **G**OALS
STAYING **L**ASER-**F**OCUSED
SELLING **Y**OUR **V**ALUE
INVIGORATING **Y**OURSELF
OMITTING THE **N**EGATIVE
NAILING THE **B**RAND

All the passion in the world won't enable you to achieve success if you employ an outdated, stale approach to your career, which is why I make sure to put "Fresh" first!

Following the Fresh PASSION methodology, I've come a long way since then. I've spent time working on the front lines, consulting with customer service managers, business unit leaders, directors, department heads, regional managers, and frontline managers in a diverse set of companies, organizations, and industries. Physically, I left the front line behind, but I have since been able to successfully infuse what I've learned and my detailed understanding of how to achieve personal and professional success despite any odds into the various roles, responsibilities, and positions I have had at a number of companies and organizations, such as Murphy Oil (The Wal-Mart Project), USF&G Insurance, BP, Marriott, ARCO, Romano's Macaroni Grill, Landry's Seafood, U.S. Army, Wells Fargo Financial, San Francisco Foundation,

Ford Foundation, Amoco, Wendy's International, Ralph & Kacoo's, and in working with a number of small independent business owners, colleges, and universities.

I have been able to wow audiences as a spokesperson in corporate videos and live television appearances, and as a trainer, commentator, coach, lecturer, and keynote speaker. But it's thanks to the Fresh PASSION that has been burning inside me since my days as a mistreated child handyman that I have been able to reach these heights and become known as the management expert who delivers fresh results.

Early in my professional career, I started working in large Fortune 100 companies. I found myself bombarded with overly prescriptive program initiatives, lofty sales goals, budget cuts, new competition, and more aggressive competitors. Rather than collapse under the weight of all these career pressures, I took the bull by the horns and started aggressively delivering the results that I thought the companies wanted. Though I was delivering the results, my career was stagnant, and my wallet was filled with credit cards that were divided into two categories: Peter and Paul (as in using Peter to pay Paul and vice versa).

I was leading a life of personal and professional poverty with no pot of gold at the end of the rainbow. I became frustrated, bitter, and extremely angry. I blamed my university for not preparing me to land a more lucrative job, I blamed my mother for not having money to give me, I blamed my boss for not getting me promoted, and then I started blaming myself and doubting my own abilities.

I did not realize what I was doing wrong until I was sitting in a staff meeting one day and my boss announced that a colleague named Reynaldo had been promoted to a great new career position. He went on to say that Reynaldo had been chosen because of his ability to deliver results and lead people, his professionalism, and because a number of people in the organization just knew him as a well-rounded individual.

The lightbulb went on over my head. When I was in college, my dean, the faculty, hundreds of students, department chairs, and other members of the university community had a favorable impression of me and there had been a clear general understanding that I stood head and shoulders above my peers. So I thought about how I had earned their respect and came to be unanimously known by them as a standout student. It was the Fresh PASSION methodology that I had used in college.

So at that point, I started implementing the Fresh PASSION methodology in my everyday life, and shortly afterward, I had established a personal brand as a leader who delivers results through and with people and who is always offering and delivering something fresh. I initially started by just executing the programs that were given to me. However, simple execution was delivering only marginal results. I knew I could do better. I knew that something was missing; something was preventing me from moving the business further, faster.

That something was Fresh PASSION. If it didn't exist in my workplace environment, then it was incumbent on me to create and deliver it, and deliver top-notch results by doing so. What I personally put in place and continued to refine throughout my career is Michael D. Brown's Steps to Fresh PASSION that will be presented in this book.

Within each element of the PASSION methodology are 6.5 steps you need to take to make sure that each element is fulfilled, whether it is Achieving Freshness, Selling Your Value, or Invigorating Yourself. The "6.5" Step is always Make it Real and Keep it Fresh. This final half step will help you get out there and make sure that you maximize your potential. Each chapter also offers a plan of action that you will create based on what you've learned by completing the process.

I made a personal commitment to myself during my high school years that I wouldn't allow the typical correlation between poverty and failure to dictate my future. I dared to beat the odds by staying focused on my hopes, dreams, and aspirations. In all the Fortune 100 and 500 companies, mid-sized organizations, and mom-and-pop stores for which I have worked, I have gone above and beyond simply executing programs and initiatives. In each of these companies, I have been recognized for my commitment to employees and to the customers, and for achieving unprecedented bottom-line results.

All this from a guy who grew up in rural Mississippi—a place that at the time of my youth was ranked at the top of almost all categories for health problems. Statistically, there was a greater chance I would struggle in my poverty-ridden county's cycle of destitution than I would achieve a successful career. Instead of a highly successful business professional, I'd be a drug addict, an absent father, or a criminal. But I beat the odds.

Now I am known by many of my colleagues, peers, friends, and employees as a leader who can consistently deliver competitive results, a leader who truly believes in developing and growing people, someone who constantly invests in his personal and professional development so that he stays fresh and competitive, and someone who is able to offer fresh sustainable solutions and ideas by going several layers beneath any problem.

If you yearn to build a successful personal brand that will allow you to reach your full potential in your career and at home, read this Fresh Green Book. This book does not contain failed complex theories on achieving success or "feel good" pop psychology. Nor does this book contain complex formulas, trade secrets, or any other "proprietary" generic fluff that some so-called experts like to peddle. I have avoided all the stale hooey, opting for Fresh PASSION that allows you to create a successful personal brand. I have used real solutions that affect real people and deliver real results.

What you will find in the following pages is a guy who is passionate about people—all types of people. The time to build your brand is NOW, so you can sell your valuable brand to a company that will make you a competitive offer.

I purposely wrote this book because Fresh PASSION is about now; it's about building a successful personal brand now. For too long, you have been struggling to figure out what you can do *now* to ensure success later and wondering why you haven't been doing better. It's not that you aren't capable or deserving, it's that you haven't marshaled your resources in a way that conveys incredible personal value to the world around you. All that is about to change.

It's never too soon to create a personal brand that will allow you to achieve the kind of success you desire and deserve. Come along and enjoy the *fresh* journey!

acknowledgments

Searching deep into my DNA to unearth all of this content and put it on paper has been a challenging and rewarding journey. I am extremely grateful for the push and tremendous support of my family, staff, friends, colleagues, and a host of cheerleaders who have planted fertile seeds in me and helped me blossom into the individual and successful professional I am today. What I have sought to do all my life and in this book is keep these seeds watered and producing life's fresh green crops.

More specifically, I'd like to thank my mom, Ella, who taught me to always have unwavering faith, confidence, and tenacity. I continue to be amazed at her strength and perseverance.

Beverly Malloy, one of my greatest supporters and critics, continues to remind me of my potential and challenges me to stretch, deliver results, and always reach further.

Laverne Y. Lindsey had an enormous impact on my childhood and well into my adult life. Though she didn't exactly call it developing and protecting your brand, she instilled in me early that I needed to protect my name and always strive for excellence in everything that I pursued. She told me early on "you have not arrived until you have reached back and helped someone." I still hear her voice to this day and it reminds me of the importance of servant leadership. The thought of her early Saturday morning lectures on speaking proper English still brings a smile to my face (though at the time I thought it was torture).

Anthony Caruth is a former frontline employee of mine and a great supporter and protector of my brand. He is always ensuring that my company and I stay on the cutting edge and take it to the next level.

Francisco O. Bennett, whom I initially contracted to design a logo for my company years ago, had no idea I am sure that a simple two-week project would expand into a working relationship that continues to this day. Francisco's unwavering commitment and long, hard working hours have helped me to shape my brands, Fresh Results and Fresh Customer Service, into something that will benefit the world. Francisco is the protector of my personal brand and that of my company. I am so fortunate to have such a passionate team member.

Sis. Beverly Weidner, Sis. Louise McKigney, and Sis. Loretta Beyer have been my godparents for almost three decades. They instilled in me early on that my brand should be rooted in integrity, authenticity, respect for mankind, and a commitment to serve others.

My ten brothers and sisters put an enormous amount of pressure on me to be the best, make the most money, and always have abundance. This drove me to the "overachiever" category.

Thank you to Paige Stover Hague Esq. and George Kasparian Esq. of the Ictus Initiative. They were believers in my brand early on and were always willing to go above and beyond to assist. It was actually Paige's idea (command, actually,) that I pen a book on what has enabled me to have a successful career inside and outside of corporate America.

High regards and thanks to my editor, Daniel E. Berthiaume, who has been with me for several years. Daniel is the only person who can effectively deal with my globe-trotting travel schedule, fast talking, long hours, juggling multiple projects at one time and the visions that come during my morning runs, my Starbucks visits, and the late night sessions.

Thanks to the thousands of individuals, companies, organizations, military branches, and direct reports of mine who trusted my leadership and guidance as I helped to create, develop, launch, and elevate their personal brands. I am amazed every day at the fresh success stories. I am greater because of you—thank you!

Thanks to Clint Greenleaf and the amazing team of professionals at Greenleaf Book Group—you are a first-class team!

And last, but by no means least, I want to extend a warm and fresh thank you to you, the reader. Thank you for coming along on this Fresh PASSION journey. I hope you have extracted tangible and timely solutions that will help you create, develop, enhance, and execute your personal brand with Fresh PASSION. I look forward to continuing the journey with you.

about this fresh green book . . .

My goal in writing this book was to provide a fun, easy-to-read, yet highly informative instruction manual on how to build a personal brand that will allow you to achieve your maximum potential at work, at home, and in all other areas of life. This Fresh Green Book is a handy size that can be read on the go. Each chapter opens up with a fresh quote.

Throughout the book, you will find "Brownie Points," real-life stories that I have personally experienced and lived to retell. They are meant to serve as parables, illustrative stories to help humanize the concepts and theories behind Fresh PASSION. It is one thing to tell you to Aspire to Reach Your Goals, it is another to show you how Aspiration actually works through examples from my personal history. To protect the innocent, I have changed the names of certain real-life people and institutions that I mention in my Brownie Points stories.

The Brownie Points are stories drawn primarily from my professional career that reflect the focus of Fresh PASSION. This book is meant to inspire and motivate you, whether you are an employee who aspires to more or already an executive or business owner, to build a competitive personal brand while equipping you with the proven and powerful tools you need to build and execute your brand.

The sooner you build that competitive personal brand, the sooner you will begin to reap the benefits and build branding equity, which will lead to greater success faster. We live in an interactive age, and I have attempted to make this book as interactive as possible. After all, I can show you how to build your brand, but I can't actually create it for you!

You've got to do that yourself, and worksheets located throughout the book will help you get on your way.

The *Your Perfect Day Worksheet™* is the foundation document for the brand-building process that will follow. I will ask you: "In five years, what will your perfect day look like—personally and professionally?" Answering this question is of vital importance, because everything you do throughout the rest of the book is filtered through the goal of making this perfect day into a reality. This worksheet sets up the target you are aiming for, and you will need to revisit it at each new stage in your life.

The *6.5 Fresh Steps*® are the tools you'll need to implement each element of the Fresh PASSION approach. In each chapter, after introducing a new element, I give you six steps that will enable you to implement that element or achieve that mindset. This is solid, practical advice that is the meat of each chapter, where I give you the tools to make it happen. The final 6.5 Step is always your reminder to "Make it Real and Keep it Fresh"—keeping you aware that this is an ongoing process that must always be updated and kept current if you want to stay competitive.

Take Your Pulse is the self-assessment portion of each chapter. After a chapter introduces a new PASSION element, explains how it works, and gives the 6.5 steps to implement it, you are invited to stop and put your fingers on the pulse of your efforts regarding this element. You are asked a series of questions that will allow you to score yourself and see exactly how healthy and robust your achievement in developing mastery of this element is. The questions can always be repeated after you have tried to implement the lessons learned in the 6.5 steps, so you can see how you have improved.

It's Showtime! is another practical tool I am giving you that will help you keep on track. It's a series of daily, weekly, monthly, quarterly, and yearly steps that you can follow to help you implement the elements of my methodology. These changes can't all be made at once, and here in the *It's Showtime!* section, I provide you with a short-term and a longer-term plan for implementing the 6.5 steps for each element in a consistent way.

The *Fresh Technologies* tools accompany each element of the Fresh PASSION process as well. They are tools I have researched—technological advances, software, and hardware that will help you in your personal brand development efforts. Each chapter offers advice on a technology that will help make that element easier to incorporate into your life.

The *Brownie Bites* are ways to interact electronically with me, either with forms that accompany each step in the Fresh PASSION process (which are available for download at www.MyFreshBrand.com) or a chance to email me samples of your branding attempts, which I will personally critique.

A *Doggie Bag* is what you use to take home the part of your dinner you could not eat in one sitting. Here I am using the Doggie Bag as a final summary at the end of each chapter of the takeaways—or the absolutely indispensable items in each chapter that I want to be sure you take home, no matter what.

Finally, with the *closing worksheet*, I will have you sum up your personal branding efforts so that you are positioned to take the next step. I will ask you to write your 10-second text messages and 30-second Super Bowl commercials (originally found in chapter 6, "Selling Your Value") and reiterate your perfect day—and then you will take your efforts to the next level. You will develop a personal logo based on your brand, a brand statement, and a business card based on your logo—keeping an eye on brand consistency all the while.

No two brands are alike, and Fresh PASSION can be applied to any type of brand. The brand of a successful salesperson and the brand of a successful research scientist will look quite different, but both are built on the same essential precepts that are key to success of any type in any field. So no matter what your goals are, get ready to meet and exceed them with confidence and yes, passion. On with the brand!

Oh, and a side note on why this book refers to the colors red and green. Red is the color of passion. It is the color associated with excitement, action, and adventure. Building your brand will involve plenty of all three—nobody ever went out and carved his or her own success by sitting at home quietly! And green is the color of freshness. It is the color associated with life, renewal, and natural health. You don't just want to "go green" in how you conserve energy or follow a nutritious diet—you want to "go green" in how you maintain an innovative, energetic approach to your life and your career. So enjoy the freshness and feel the passion!

1
GET A BRAND OR DIE A GENERIC®

Quotable Notables: Peter Drucker, Steve Jobs

Brownie Point: My Life as a Frontline Prisoner

Your Perfect Day Worksheet

Become a Distinct and Competitive Brand or an Extinct Generic

A Brief Summary of Personal Branding

> *"Success in the knowledge economy comes to those who know themselves—their strengths, their values, and how they best perform."*
>
> —PETER F. DRUCKER (1909–2005)
>
> *"Be a yardstick of quality. Some people aren't used to an environment where excellence is expected."*
>
> —STEVE JOBS (1955–2011)

QUOTABLE NOTABLES: PETER DRUCKER AND STEVE JOBS

Peter Drucker was a highly regarded business thinker who popularized the term "knowledge worker" and helped major corporations such as General Motors adapt their organizational structure to the knowledge economy, which took root after World War II. He understood that business was increasingly relying upon the talents and capabilities of individuals.

Steve Jobs was one of the original founders of Apple, one of the world's most successful and innovative technology brands. Always known as a maverick thinker, Jobs resigned in the mid-1980s to found NeXT Computer, a company whose technology was critical to developing the World Wide Web. Jobs rejoined Apple in the late 1990s and helped the then-struggling company achieve unprecedented success with products such as the iMac, iPod, and iPhone. Jobs was a true visionary whose aspirations allowed him to succeed despite significant obstacles and have benefited the entire world through technological advancement. His name still has the ability to inspire innovation and create customer experiences that are unmatched. Through innovation and a tireless focus on delivering a unique customer experience, Jobs took what otherwise would have been a generic high-technology company and turned it into a lifestyle accessory for hip, computer-savvy people, especially those in the creative fields.

BROWNIE POINT: MY LIFE AS A FRONTLINE PRISONER

I would like to share with you the story of my difficult time as a multiunit manager of frontline employees at a Fortune 500 company I will refer to as "Majestic Suites," a period I like to call my "frontline prisoner" days. I think this story is a great example of both why Fresh PASSION is so important and how it can make the difference between having a dead-end career and having a career that maximizes your professional and personal potential and allows you to realize your perfect day (more on that shortly).

Remember, when your brand is stale and dull, it will sit ignored in the marketplace while "consumers" (i.e., the people who will ultimately determine how well you succeed) will fight over the fresher, more exciting brands that are available. By the time someone selects your brand, out of desperation, lack of choice, or budgetary constraints, you will have died a generic death.

As I will explain in detail, the Majestic Suites unit at the Little Rock International Airport had fallen into disarray and was not representative of what you would expect when you enter a business that is a perennial member of the Fortune 500.

After about a week on the job, the other managers and assistant managers started to tell me about how things really worked at the airport. This was after I signed an oath in blood that I wouldn't tell the unit's general manager, a man I will refer to as Mr. Wallace Wright. A small sampling of the problems I heard about included a 400 percent turnover rate, ethical issues, several quarters of missed sales targets, expenses that were 30 percent over budget, and customer satisfaction scores that were in the toilet. We were using a temporary agency on a permanent basis to staff the stores and concessions.

Wallace (all these years later I still cringe at referring to him on a first-name basis, as if we were buddies) wanted us to increase sales and customer satisfaction scores, and most important, slow the bleeding with employee turnover, including the temporary employees who were leaving at an alarming rate. I was certainly up for the challenge and believed that I could help turn things around.

After about a month on the job, employees started regularly coming to me and saying things like, "Michael, you are much too smart to be working here, why are you here . . . you can do so much better someplace else." I was determined to make a difference, despite Wallace's authoritarian, heavy-handed style. He came to me one day and stated that I had the highest sales and the employees liked working with me. Despite this positive comment, I was still determined to get myself out of this situation. These were some of the darkest days of my life.

Wallace said in a staff meeting that the employees complained that they couldn't get assistance from any manager except Michael, but he didn't ask what I was doing to assist them. He stated that my sales were 40 percent higher but did not ask how I got them that way.

Instead, he said the employees didn't up-sell, didn't take care of the customers in a timely manner, and were not happy when I wasn't at work. He went on to say that I should be training employees to perform at all times, even when they were working for other managers, and that I was a poor leader. I started to tell him how I motivated people and how I ran my shifts differently, which was a BIG mistake.

Wallace quickly stopped me and said that I didn't have authority to change the way things were done and that he was the general manager. He further said that I was being insubordinate. Though he liked the results I was getting, he didn't want to hear how I was getting the results. At this point, I just became confused and concluded that I needed to walk on eggshells with Wallace and just sing his praises.

I realized early on that if I wanted to deliver the financial and human results that would make me personally proud and get me noticed by the outside world (at this time I was trying to get promoted to an assistant GM position at the St. Louis airport), I needed to do this through and with the frontline employees.

I also realized that I needed to train them, set the expectations, provide them with tools, empower them, motivate them, inspire them, and genuinely care about them while at the same time hold them accountable to delivering a world-class customer experience. I further realized that Wallace was only concerned about the bottom-line number and cared very little about the frontline employees or customers.

So I went on and operated within the box while Wallace was around, but while he wasn't around I did the "extra" stuff that motivated, empowered, and excited the front line, which in turn delivered a world-class customer service experience and bottom-line numbers that Wallace couldn't deny were good. You have to quickly realize which battles are worth fighting and which ones you need to concede to on the surface.

This experience proved to be a tremendous building block for my personal brand. I learned that, sometimes, to deliver the lofty goals and results prescribed by your manager/leader, you need to be creative and ensure that the manager's ego and quest for power is not damaged.

This can lead to confrontations that will distract you from growing your personal brand (in this case it was me attempting to build on my track record of getting results through and with people) and achieving the goals of the business, and may ultimately lead to career suicide. So I marched to Wallace's orders while building my arsenal, skills, competencies, and brand equity in preparation for other opportunities that might exist internally and externally. I gained the trust and respect of thoroughly discouraged and demoralized frontline employees—no small feat. More important, despite the best efforts of Mr. Wallace Wright to obscure my accomplishments, I was able to build some brand equity that would pay handsome dividends both personally and professionally on the open market. I was able to eloquently and boldly speak of this brand equity I had built during an interview for a field manager role with Amoco Oil Company (a Fortune 5 company).

During the interview, I was able to draw on the experiences at my previous role with Majestic Suites and speak about my leadership style that gets results through and with people and how this translates to a more productive and excited workforce, increased customer satisfaction, and a double-digit increase to the bottom line.

I was then able to tell the interview panel how I could take this experience and provide even greater returns for Amoco. They realized that an investment in me would yield a great return for them. Out of sixteen candidates, I was offered the role. Thank you, Mr. Wallace Wright, for taking me through hell in preparation for a heavenly assignment!

As you can see, by maintaining a fresh approach to my job as a frontline manager and retaining my passion for my brand even in the face of overwhelming negativity and hostility from Wallace Wright, I was able to escape a situation that could have killed my career before it even really started. That would have doomed me to a generic death as a result of having my brand development squelched and I would have become known as another guy who went into a difficult situation, tried his best, and failed. This illustrates another important lesson about building your brand—you must build it, even if others are trying to tear it down, or you will die generic. Don't sit back and assume your hard work will be recognized, make sure it is visible for miles around!

YOUR PERFECT DAY WORKSHEET

If I had allowed my working environment to sap my will to succeed at a level hardly anyone would have dreamed possible, I would have remained a low-level manager under the suffocating thumb of Wallace Wright. I never would have built the brand I possess today and would probably still be stuck as a frontline manager in the Little Rock airport location of Majestic Suites, earning low pay, hating my job, and generally watching my career die a slow, generic death as I "topped out" at that level by never proving myself worthy of doing something more challenging, interesting, and rewarding. Instead, I have followed the principles of Fresh PASSION and built a brand that has allowed me to enjoy a tremendous amount of personal and professional success, and I live something close to what I would consider my perfect day.

Your perfect day is what you should be striving to achieve through the fresh personal brand you build. Imagine how your typical day would proceed if you were able to realize every major personal and professional goal you hold and you had full control over every aspect of your life. You may never fully achieve it, but by keeping your perfect day in mind, you create a concrete target at which you can aim your brand-building efforts. And even if you do fully realize your perfect day, a key part of Fresh PASSION is never being satisfied to rest on your past accomplishments, so it's time to develop an even more perfect "perfect day" to strive toward!

Complete the following worksheet exercise to determine exactly what kind of day you want to be living. I have also included my own perfect day worksheet to give you an example of the kinds of goals you may want to strive for. But don't feel constrained by what I say; this is *your* perfect day stemming from *your* brand—there are no right or wrong answers, and no two perfect days will be alike!

Write Your PERFECT DAY Five Years From Now

This is a day where you can wake up and say, "Wow, I have achieved my desired personal and professional success and I am going to keep going and do even better!"

If you are like me you just might want to type this on a computer and print it out instead of handwriting it (I am still learning how to read my own handwriting).

Now let's get started, and don't leave out any of the small details. Be sure to think as large and as globally as you like. Here are some questions to consider and answer: What does your family look like? What's your financial picture? What are you doing professionally? What does your personal life look like? What does personal and professional success look like? Are you an entrepreneur? Are you working in a corporation? Are you employed inside your home? Where do you vacation? Do you own real estate? Do you have a favorite cause/charity that you are giving back to? What are your credentials?

_____

_____

_____

_____

_____

_____

_____

_____

_____

_____

_____

You can download this form at www.MyFreshBrand.com.

Michael D. Brown's Perfect Day Five Years From Now

- I am debt free, using the earnings of my investments to support and finance my lifestyle, foundation, business, and further personal, professional growth/goals.
- I am staying fresh with specialty and advanced training, certifications, and credentialing in my area of branded expertise.
- God is still the center and is still working through me.
- My personal and professional success continues to accelerate and stay fresh—I'm forever growing both personally and professionally.
- I am fully engaged in my personal and professional success and in total alignment: physically, mentally, emotionally, and spiritually.
- I am speaking for Fortune 500 companies and business schools.
- My daily investment fee for clients has increased 55 percent and I am delivering 55 percent more return on their investment.
- I am delivering and driving fresh results through and with people while offering a unique experience. This work is underpinned by my Fresh Customer Service® and Fresh PASSION tools and processes. The main focus here is to help individuals, organizations, and companies achieve exponential personal, professional, and economic growth. This work has a coaching, speaking, training, and seminar component. I have completed the books on Fresh Customer Service (done!) and Fresh PASSION (you are reading it now).
- The Get a Brand or Die a Generic program has expanded to a full executive coaching, training, and seminar enterprise.
- This feels really good, because I am working in my destiny and doing what I am passionate about and I am making a difference in the lives of individuals and in organizations.

- I have opened the Fresh Results Institute and am serving 1,000 participants.
- I have a Ritz-Carlton vacation home in Florida.
- I have a slate of products centered around Fresh Customer Service and Get a Brand or Die a Generic. This includes books, manuals, audio, teleseminars, online courses, and other training materials.
- My personal relationship has been strengthened with my family—I am spending the holidays with them and I am taking them on an all-expenses-paid vacation once a year.
- My health is in tip-top shape, and I am still working out.
- I have started the Michael D. Brown Foundation.

BECOME A DISTINCT AND COMPETITIVE BRAND OR AN EXTINCT GENERIC

The world is changing, as is the economy. It is no secret that for the past few years, we have been in the midst of what can only be termed an "economic tsunami."

Companies, organizations, customers, your colleagues, and your boss all expect more—and with unemployment at new highs, it's more important than ever to distinguish yourself. Your customers and employers expect you to provide an experience that is different from what your competition is offering. They want an experience that adds more value. They want an experience that fulfills a particular need, want, or desire, and you have to figure out how to give it to them.

So if they see you as a "generic," then you're in trouble. You've seen generic brands, the "no-name" products that usually sit low on the supermarket shelves. For the most part, they're not that radically different from the costlier name brands placed directly at eye-level—in fact, the very same companies that make those name brands often make the generics as well! But whether it's due to their dull packaging, lack of promotion, or simple fact they are less recognizable to the typical consumer, generic products typically sit on the shelves for a long period of time, only picked up by someone looking for a short-term bargain. People expect to and do pay less for generic!

Guess what? People can be generic, too. What is a generic person? Simply put, a generic person is someone who may be perfectly nice, intelligent, and talented, but who hasn't made any effort to stand out from the crowd. They probably went to an average school, got average grades, and have an average work history and personal background. They don't stand out as being especially bad, but don't really stand out as being especially good, either. You could call them your average working stiffs.

What's wrong with the average working stiff, you may ask? Nothing, on a purely humanistic level. All people are created equal. But after creation is where the equality ends. In today's competitive, roller coaster world, you're either a *distinct and competitive brand or an extinct generic.*

As a result of the economic tsunami we have all been struggling to navigate through, personal, economic, and professional success seems to be sinking to anemic levels. But the tsunami doesn't have to determine the outcome of your life and/or career. For example, I was able to grow and prosper during what have so far been the very darkest days of the continuing economic "weather emergency": the 2009 global recession/downturn/spiraling-out-of-control economy. In these stormy times, you, too, can survive, prosper, and achieve great success, but you must become a distinct and competitive personal brand (yes, you need to *become* a personal brand).

When you develop this brand, you will be able to deliver the experience that people are willing to subscribe to and/or pay for. Then, you can take yourself, your colleagues, your organizations, and your employers, your customers, your students, or your members to a new level.

In writing this book, I seek to challenge you to:

- Think different.
- Be different.
- Do different.
- See different.
- Brand different.

Think about "brand-name" celebrities like Michael Jordan, Lady Gaga, Oprah Winfrey, Ryan Seacrest, Magic Johnson, or even Eminem! These people all function as personal brands, but they weren't built overnight and they constantly evolve to stay fresh in the mind of the consumer. Like these and other celebrities whose fame has transcended their identities as mere humans, you want to build a brand for yourself that screams fresh, passionate, determined, different, skilled, and competitive!

Naturally, there is a lot more to building a successful personal brand than waking up in the morning and saying, "I'd like to become a personal brand today." Like anything else worthwhile in life, it takes time, passion, skill, and determination. As mentioned in the preface, I have developed a methodology called Fresh PASSION, which is an acronym for:

PREPARING **Y**OURSELF
ASPIRING TO **R**EACH **Y**OUR **G**OALS
STAYING **L**ASER-**F**OCUSED
SELLING **Y**OUR **V**ALUE
I NVIGORATING **Y**OURSELF
OMITTING THE **N**EGATIVE
NAILING THE **B**RAND

What does each of these terms actually mean?

Chapter by chapter, this book will explain each one in detail, using examples from my own successful career to illustrate how by mastering every step of the Fresh PASSION methodology you can gear your career and your entire life to generate the kind of personal and professional success that, up until now, you have only dared to dream of. Dreams can become real, if you know how to make them happen and are willing to put in the time and effort!

A BRIEF SUMMARY OF PERSONAL BRANDING

This entire book is about branding yourself. Some of you may be wondering what exactly "personal branding" means. It's okay, don't be embarrassed, you'd be surprised how many people who think they understand personal branding really don't!

Your personal brand is that solid and consistent impression that comes to mind when people think of you. Think about it this way; it is the mental picture that is invoked when your name is mentioned.

The first step in creating a personal brand is identifying your target audience/market. Is it a company who can award you a job with a six-figure potential? A future employer who will appoint you to your dream role? Whatever the case, figure out who you are targeting.

Now find out what this person's or organization's needs and wants are, and then quickly determine if you can meet their needs or wants. Next, you need to create reasons people should believe you will deliver the results that your brand promises.

In short, figure out the pain (needs/wants) that exists for the person or organization, and show them how you can solve their pain via the brand that you possess. For example, let's say a company wants an employee who has a track record of delivering results. You have a track record of delivering results, and it's a part of your brand. You know the pain the company is feeling and you have the solution . . . you will probably get hired!

Now here is the competitive part—figure out what makes you different from your competitors. When you create this personal brand identity, you will be sought after as the person who can meet the particular needs of a company. YOU HAVE TO STAND OUT.

Think about it this way. It's a win-win situation for the company, organization, firm, etc., and you. If you are a strong, competitive brand, your ROI (return on investment) to the company is greater. So guess what? Since they benefit more from you, they are willing to pay more and work harder to get you and retain you.

This also works if you are trying to obtain a promotion or move up the ranks. Think about it—you know who the top performers are in your organization. You know friends and colleagues who are just standout people, attracting customers, employment opportunities, etc. Throughout the book, I will give you examples from my own career where building a successful personal brand allowed me to obtain the kind of leadership positions, promotions, and professional contacts that are still paying dividends in my career and personal life many years after I entered the job market.

In conclusion, this whole concept of personal branding is fairly new and has picked up some steam over the last several years. It is what successful people are doing to manage their careers and businesses. Put simply, personal branding is a method whereby you precisely lay out and clearly communicate what makes you different and unique. Then, you take this uniqueness and difference and distance yourself from your competition (your peers) so that you can accelerate your success while continuing to refresh the brand so that it stays fresh and competitive. Once you clearly understand your brand, you are positioned to express the benefits and values to your target audience, no matter who it may be.

Does that all make sense? It soon will, and the results will speak for themselves. Get ready for the biggest positive change your life has ever seen. Your personal brand already exists. It is up to you to locate it, define it, and broadcast it to the world. The alternative, dying a generic death as a result of failing to put the necessary work into building and broadcasting your brand, is simply not an option any success-oriented person would entertain for even a moment.

2

ACHIEVING FRESHNESS

Quotable Notable: Oprah Winfrey

Brownie Point: Side-by-Side Walking for a Fresh Perspective

Freshness: The Concept, Rationale, and Importance

6.5 Fresh Steps toward Achieving Freshness

- **Achieving Freshness: Step 1**—Establish a network, refresh your network.
- **Achieving Freshness: Step 2**—Identify three of the most successful people in the area of branded expertise that you are going to capture.
- **Achieving Freshness: Step 3**—Research what your successful people do to stay fresh.
- **Achieving Freshness: Step 4**—Implement five fresh steps into your daily routine.
- **Achieving Freshness: Step 5**—Sign up for RSS or other feeds of current information.
- **Achieving Freshness: Step 6**—Become an expert with supporting technologies.
- **Achieving Freshness: Step 6.5**—Make it Real and Keep it Fresh—Communicating Freshness.

Take Your Pulse: Self-assessment questions measuring your freshness efforts

It's Showtime!: Develop the need to maintain freshness and take daily, weekly, monthly, quarterly, and yearly steps to put your plan into action

Fresh Technologies: iPods & Podcasting, Smartphones and Tablets, Internet Phone Calls, Web Conferencing

Brownie Bite

The Doggie Bag: The Achieving Freshness Takeaways

> *"My philosophy is that not only are you responsible for your life, but doing the best at this moment puts you in the best place for the next moment."*
>
> —OPRAH WINFREY

QUOTABLE NOTABLE: OPRAH WINFREY

One of the world's most famous, powerful, and wealthy women, Oprah Winfrey rose from a dysfunctional, impoverished background to become an entrepreneur who hosted one of the most popular talk shows in history, runs her own cable TV network, publishes a self-titled magazine, operates a satellite radio channel, and is involved in numerous other business and charity ventures. By always trying to achieve something significant with her business and charitable activities, Oprah has built a personal brand that inspires trust, loyalty, and devotion from millions of fans across the globe. On a side note, Oprah originally hails from Kosciusko, Mississippi, down the road from where I grew up, further proof that it's not where you start in life that matters, but where you end up!

BROWNIE POINT: SIDE-BY-SIDE WALKING FOR A FRESH PERSPECTIVE

Realizing the power of freshness in college, after graduating I took it into corporate America, where I made the ability to deliver fresh results a cornerstone of my brand. This cornerstone ignited and continues to fuel my personal and professional success. Let me tell you a story about how I helped an organization figure out the problem and offered a fresh, winning solution.

At a certain fast-paced retail chain—I'll protect its real identity and call it "Chips n Sips"—declining sales were the source of sleepless nights, headaches, and heated arguments among the increasingly frustrated leadership team. The company's marketing experts finally put their heads together and decided to implement a new cross-selling program that they introduced to all the employees with great fanfare.

The program used colorful, attention-grabbing printed marketing materials. To help cashiers with their new cross-selling task, managers provided a set of bookmark-sized laminated "cheat cards" with several items to suggest.

These cards were placed at all Chips n Sips registers to remind the cashiers what items to cross-sell with each purchase. If a customer bought milk, the cashier was to offer her bread (the laminated cards showed a picture of a milk carton with an arrow pointing to a loaf of bread). If another customer bought beer, the cashier was to suggest chips (same picture format). The cashiers started to follow this procedure but soon became discouraged by the number of rejections they were experiencing.

The bread being cross-sold with the milk was located several feet away from the checkout stand, likewise for the chips being cross-sold with the beer. Customers were reluctant to give up their spots in line to go pick up the suggested items—we all know how more than a few minutes in line are unacceptable to today's shopper. The handful of customers who decided to get out of line and return with a cross-sold item were greeted by the other customers' looks of hatred and disgust for holding up the line.

In short, this cross-selling program was a disaster. It held up the lines and de-motivated the cashiers because of non-stop rejections. If the marketers and senior managers had been more in touch with the layout of the stores, the way cashiers operated, and customers' shopping styles, they would have understood this promotional method was doomed from the get-go. This futile attempt at boosting sales ended up costing Chips n Sips more than $100,000 in marketing and promotional costs.

I knew there had to be a better way to do this, so when Chips n Sips hired me as a consultant to help grow their business and the efficiency and effectiveness of their frontline employees, one of my first contributions to the business was offering a fresh cross-selling process based on a completely different strategy. Before I offered any ideas, I first went to a local Chips n Sips outlet and took note of how registers were set up, where products were located in the store, and what cashiers had to do during the failed cross-selling program.

While this may seem like the commonsense first step, you'd be amazed how few companies actually do any real site-level research before launching new strategies that will impact the experience of their customers and/or frontline employees. Sometimes the fresh approach involves seeing things in a radically different light, and sometimes it involves simply seeing things the way they are!

This fresh insider's look at the business helped me develop a plan. I began by asking a Chips n Sips store manager to select a special item to promote each day. Every morning, that day's item was placed in a basket next to the register, and the cashiers simply had to cross-sell the item located at arm's length on the checkout stand. This way, customers could continue checking out without having to get out of line.

After following this process for three weeks, we began to ask frontline employees to select an item. You can only imagine how fast the items selected by the frontline employees sold. You guessed right; it was easy for them to sell a product that they liked and believed in. The cashiers received 54 percent fewer rejections.

Side-by-side walking, which I like to describe as walking a mile in the shoes of employees to understand what they do, how they do it, and how they experience their jobs, would have helped the Chips n Sips leadership team tremendously. It didn't take me much time to visit a store and see for myself why the less-than-stellar cross-selling program was self-destructing right before their eyes.

If the marketing managers themselves had taken the time to go out and see how difficult it was for cashiers to cross-sell a product, making a customer wait in line longer and be the recipient of scowls from other customers, they never would have implemented their cross-selling program. Side-by-side walking would have prevented the original difficulties with the cross-selling program because the marketing department would have understood the importance of customer flow and the negative impact constant rejections would have on frontline employee morale.

Side-by-side walking is a perfect example of how freshness lurks everywhere. The person you may be tempted to ignore or dismiss, like the cashier, maintenance person, or customer running into a convenience store to grab a jug of milk on the way home from work, likely holds incredible value and insight. You just have to have your "fresh antennae" on and be attuned enough to the endless fresh possibilities that exist in this wide world of ours to pick up on that value and insight.

Trust me, most of your competitors are too busy focusing on their own narrow interests or trying to follow complex management theories they learned in grad school to ever think of a fresh approach like side-by-side walking. Chips n Sips greatly improved its value proposition to customers and obtained fresh profits and market share by using side-by-side walking. And over the years, the value I have delivered to dozens of companies through side-by-side walking exercises has helped me build my own fresh personal brand, which has allowed me to experience an enormous level of personal and professional success, while staying focused on staying fresh so that I am competitive and poised to capture ever-greater personal success.

FRESHNESS: THE CONCEPT, RATIONALE, AND IMPORTANCE

Putting the handle "Fresh" before "PASSION" is critically important, because without a fresh approach to your career and your life, all the PASSION in the world will likely not be able to help you achieve your fullest potential. You can't just land your newly developed brand today, put it on a shelf, and expect it to carry you throughout your professional career while you sit back and reap its rewards.

Anyone who has ever been in love (or even thought they were in love) can attest to this. The initial courtship is passionate, and you can't see enough of each other. But as you know, time goes on, competition enters, and that once-passionate flame begins to turn into a flicker that eventually burns out. If a relationship is to have any chance of thriving long term, you've got to keep it fresh, right?

That same analogy is true for companies. In companies needs change, strategic direction changes, the type of employee they are looking for changes, the skill sets they are looking for changes, economic factors change, and customer needs change (especially important for entrepreneurs and companies in the customer-facing business). You need to stay fresh to be in tip-top competitive shape. Staying fresh provides you with a greater ROI for the employer than that from a potential employee who has just kept pace with the status quo.

The same is true for entrepreneurs; customers want products and services that are fresh and they want the delivery vehicle (the people). In essence, they want world-class products, services, and customer experience.

Do something every day to enhance your brand so that it stays fresh. Would you rather buy fresh bread or old bread? Trust me, employers would rather hire employees who have stayed fresh: ones who have kept up with the times, kept their skills sharpened, developed a set of skills and attributes that will deliver an outstanding ROI, are packaged well, continue to invest in their personal brands, and have maintained a competitive edge. And if you are planning to become an entrepreneur, you will find that customers and clients would much rather deal with a business whose products, services, and capabilities reflect the most current needs of the marketplace.

6.5 FRESH STEPS TOWARD ACHIEVING FRESHNESS

Okay, so it's easy for me to sit here at my keyboard and type out advice on the importance of being and staying fresh. I've explained to you what freshness is, why it's so important in today's educational arena and job market, and even provided you with a real-life example of how freshness works. But now that you know all about freshness, how are you supposed to go out into the world and make it happen?

Fortunately for you, I have distilled the essence of achieving freshness into 6.5 steps that are easy to understand and implement. Don't misunderstand me when I say "easy" to implement—a lot of effort and passion on your part will be required to make anything happen! But these steps are easy to implement in that with the right dedication and mindset, you can incorporate them into your regular daily life without massively overhauling your existing busy schedule.

Think of it as almost like a diet—you don't have to radically change your daily life to lose weight. Most diets that require you to radically change your daily life are fad "crash" diets that may offer short-term weight loss but give almost no hope of lasting health and happiness. To achieve lifetime success with weight management, you only need to change your attitude toward eating.

Likewise, to become fresh, you need to change your attitude toward living! Rather than trying to adopt a "quick fix" to obtain pseudo-success that will not last, take the longer-term approach of developing a fresh attitude toward life that will allow you to achieve personal and professional success that permeates your entire existence.

Without further ado, let's take a walk through each of the 6.5 steps:

- *Achieving Freshness: Step 1*
  Establish a network, refresh your network.

- *Achieving Freshness: Step 2*
  Identify three of the most successful people in the area of branded expertise that you are going to capture.

- *Achieving Freshness: Step 3*
  Research what your successful people do to stay fresh.

- *Achieving Freshness: Step 4*
  Implement five fresh steps into your daily routine.

- *Achieving Freshness: Step 5*
  Sign up for RSS feeds.

- *Achieving Freshness: Step 6*
  Become an expert with supporting technologies.

- *Achieving Freshness: Step 6.5*
  Make it Real and Keep it Fresh—Communicating Freshness.

Achieving Freshness: Step 1—Establish a network, refresh your network

An old adage states, "No man is an island." While this saying (which equally applies to women!) is attributed to medieval English poet John Donne, it has never been truer than it is right now in the early twenty-first century.

Simply put, without a well-established and maintained network, you will not go far in this world. You could be the most brilliant and talented person in your field, but if you lack a network of peers/colleagues/supporters/believers in the brand who can vouch for you and put you in touch with the right people, all that brilliance and talent will go unnoticed. Due to immense market pressures and the rapid speed of modern business, today's employers do not have time to waste searching for job candidates, evaluating them from scratch, and then hiring and training one they hope will turn out to be successful.

A large number of employers are now more willing to hire people they know, either directly or through someone, who can demonstrate they will succeed with a minimum of training or development. They will ask someone who knows you and is in your network what your track record is like, whether you make things happen, and whether you can get results. You want to empower your network members with the ability to respond with a resounding, "He/she is the person that can make it happen and he/she has a track record of results to prove it."

So how do you go about establishing a network? Start with the people you know. As an aspiring or current member of the professional world, hopefully you have already taken some basic network-building steps, but don't be complacent. Continue to join professional associations and volunteer for causes you believe in. Look for the "movers and shakers" and invite them into your network. Identify people who are where you want to be and are what you want to become and soak up their knowledge like a sponge. Identify the leading brand expert in your field of expertise (you will know them because everyone goes to them for advice and to make things happen). Seek out people who can help alleviate the areas where you have the greatest opportunities for improvement (aka your "weak spots").

Attend as many professional conferences and trade shows as you can, and meet as many people as possible while you're there. Within your company, serve on internal committees and focus groups, especially ones that will bring you in close contact with employees from other departments with whom you otherwise might have little interaction. Also keep in mind that a network is a living, breathing organism. It needs regular nourishment or it will die (remember, you have to keep it fresh). Refresh your network on a regular basis. Call that old college buddy you haven't seen in a while and find out what he or she is up to. A powerful phrase from the mouth of a high-performing employee to his or her boss is "Oh, he/she would be a great employee, we went to the same college and are friends." The phrase is equally important when it's uttered to a customer that you want to do business with as an entrepreneur.

Make a point of speaking out at the next meeting of your professional organization, or take a leadership role in your civic group's next fund-raiser. Demonstrate to the people in your network that you genuinely value their time and friendship and watch how much more productive your network becomes. Get connected and/or stay connected with your alumni association, and be active in as many groups and events as possible.

And one final note on networking in the twenty-first century—your network is no longer constrained by physical boundaries. Thanks to the unifying power of the Internet, you can build a virtual network that spans the globe. Professional networking sites such as LinkedIn and Spoke.com, alumni- and personal history–oriented sites such as MyLife.com, and even social networking sites such as Facebook and Twitter allow you to establish a profile and build valuable relationships with people you may never even "meet" in the physical sense! There are also numerous other sites dedicated to professions, hobbies, charities, and interests that can instantly put you in touch with like-minded peers around the world.

If you maintain any type of personal social networking profile, website, or blog, please keep in mind that it needs to reflect the type of image you want to present to prospective employers and business contacts, not the type of image you want to present to your college pals! Compromising photos are out, as are blog entries describing your alcohol intake during last weekend's big party. As a good rule of thumb—if you'd be embarrassed for your parents or kids to see it, keep it off the Internet!

Achieving Freshness: Step 2—Identify three of the most successful people in the area of branded expertise that you are going to capture

While some people like to attribute the success of others as "luck," this is really just jealousy talking. True success never occurs through simple luck. Even in the case where someone assumes control of a successful family business or inherits a large sum of money, if that person doesn't have what it takes to succeed, they will fail. Many a family business or fortune has been quickly squandered when an unqualified heir inherited the reins!

Likewise, a "lucky break" will be of no help to a person who is unwilling or unable to recognize the opportunity, seize it, and then capitalize on it to achieve success. Showbiz legend has it that the great leading man Burt Lancaster got his first big Broadway role because a casting director mistook him for another actor. Even if this is true, do you think Lancaster could have parlayed that role into a towering stage and film career if he had been a dud in front of the audience and camera?

Now that you're ready to recognize that success is never an accident, identify three of the most successful people in your area of branded expertise. Think big. Don't restrict yourself to the three most successful people who you know, or who live in your region. If you want to be a success in real estate and you live in Omaha, Nebraska, you won't do much better than making Donald Trump one of your three role models.

Achieving Freshness: Step 3—Research what your successful people do to stay fresh

You have identified three major success stories in your area of branded expertise. Now it's time to do a little homework. We live in the "Information Age," an age where the whole notion of privacy has changed and personal details of almost anyone's life can be found. We'll save the debate about the overall ethics and implications of this situation for another time. Right now, we will use it to our advantage.

Depending on whom you have identified and what field you're in, researching what they do to stay fresh could be as simple as a visit to an online search engine or informational site, a visit to a bookseller site, a trip to your local library or bookstore, or it may involve a little more legwork. To stay with the Donald Trump example, he has never been shy about trumpeting the secrets to his success for the world to hear (for a price, of course!). Trump has written numerous books about his business philosophies and strategies, and there has been at least one major biography written about him, as well. You will also find detailed biographical data and commentary on his life and career using any major search engine such as Google or informational site such as Wikipedia; although, online data always deserves an extra bit of skepticism before it is accepted as fact! Fields such as medicine and sales also contain numerous celebrity success stories that can be easily researched. Also keep in mind that even many famous and successful people are willing to put details of their lives out on the Web on social networking or personal blogging sites for everyone to see.

Naturally, if you want to enter show business or professional sports, there is no shortage of famous success stories to choose from. Keep in mind the odds against you are incredibly long and that most of the success stories you will read are of the "tell-all" variety and will likely offer as many examples of what not to do as what to do!

But what if your chosen field is less flashy? What if you seek success in something more "under the radar," such as developing industrial solvents? Not to worry. First, if you're not already reading the trade publications that cover your field of interest, start reading them. No matter how obscure your chosen career is there are at least one or two magazines dedicated to it. If you have identified top performers in your field, there will probably be information about them in those publications, even if you have to do a little digging through back issues. Also look through printed and online professional guides, such as "Who's Who" type publications, for biographical information about successful people in your field.

And don't be shy about using your network! Maybe a contact you haven't spoken to in a while went to the same alma mater as or worked alongside one of your targeted success stories. What a perfect excuse to call them up and reconnect!

Achieving Freshness: Step 4—Implement five fresh steps into your daily routine

So you've identified three successful people and researched how they stay fresh. All that information does you little good on its own. You need to do a little "modeling," which is one of the biggest secrets of successful people. Why develop a success strategy from scratch when you can crib ideas from someone who has already done it before you? The great ancient Greek philosopher Aristotle unabashedly used ideas from his teacher Socrates, and successful people have been following in the footsteps of mentors and role models ever since.

Continuing with the Donald Trump example, according to his book *Trump: The Art of the Deal* (New York: Random House, 1987), he rises most mornings by six a.m. and spends an hour reading newspapers. He arrives to work by nine a.m. and during the course of a working day that runs till about six-thirty p.m., makes 50 to 100 phone calls and has at least a dozen meetings, most of which last no longer than fifteen minutes. He rarely stops for lunch and will often continue making phone calls from home until midnight and all through the weekend. Trump finds all of this activity enjoyable.

If you are planning how you will start your career as a real estate developer, you could easily work five of these steps into your daily routine. Rise at six a.m.? Check. Spend an hour reading newspapers? Check. Arrive to work by nine? Check (come on, you should be doing this step already!). Make 50 to 100 phone calls per day? Check. Skip lunch? Check. And even if your personal schedule wouldn't allow you to make calls from home until midnight or through the weekend, you could certainly still enjoy your work as a real estate developer. Implementing these steps couldn't possibly make you *less* successful, and I'd be amazed if they didn't make you *more* successful over the long haul!

Achieving Freshness: Step 5—Sign up for RSS or other feeds of current information

RSS stands for "Really Simple Syndication," and if you don't already know what it is you need to learn, pronto! RSS is a Web feed protocol that allows content such as news updates and blog entries to be continually streamed directly to your computer or mobile device. You obtain RSS content through reader software that can be downloaded free from a variety of online sources (as with any free download, do your homework and only select software from a verified, safe provider!). A wide variety of RSS links are available for you to stream via your reader. Most major news sites offer RSS syndication, as well as blog sites, chat rooms, etc. By signing up for RSS feeds from sources relevant to your area of branded expertise, you can easily stay on top of all the latest developments and happenings without having to constantly go to the trouble of performing a manual Web search. In addition, sites including Google and Twitter allow you to sign up for email alerts, so that links to notable postings regarding a specific topic automatically arrive in your email inbox on a daily or weekly basis.

Achieving Freshness: Step 6—Become an expert with supporting technologies

Becoming and staying fresh is easier than ever, thanks to the continually expanding array of personal electronic devices that allow you to stay plugged in to your network and the world around you. In previous steps, I have touched on the fresh potential of the Internet in general and of RSS feeds in particular, but have not delved into the myriad supporting technologies that allow you to fully harness this potential, 24 hours a day, seven days a week. For more details on some of the latest and greatest technologies that are out there waiting to support your fresh efforts, see the "Fresh Technologies" section in this chapter!

Achieving Freshness: Step 6.5—Make it Real and Keep it Fresh—Communicating Freshness

After following the first six steps to freshness, it's time to take the additional "half step" of making sure that everything about you communicates and exudes freshness. Like it or not, image and appearance are extremely important, and unless you look and act the role of fresh, you can follow the first six steps to the hilt and they will get you nowhere.

To help radiate freshness to the world around you, use a simple acronym I refer to as MISS—mindset, image, skills, and substance. *Mindset* means having a mentality that focuses on freshness. When you get up in the morning, are you thinking about what you can do to be as fresh as possible in the upcoming day? Are you keeping your mind sharp and focused throughout your daily activities, even the dull, routine ones? Are you constantly engaging yourself with colleagues, bosses, friends, and strangers?

Image means projecting an aura of freshness to everyone you encounter. Are your clothes neat, clean, and in line with the latest fashion? Do you perform all the necessary daily personal hygiene and grooming steps? Is your smile wide, gaze steady, handshake firm? Do you carry an ample supply of eye-catching business cards and a quality leather attaché case to your internships and job interviews, and do you use fine personalized letterhead for all your correspondence?

Skills means having the goods to back up your fresh mindset and image. Are you constantly taking advantage of educational and professional development opportunities to stay on the cutting edge of your field? Do you volunteer for extra assignments that will keep your existing capabilities sharp and teach you new ones? Do you use personal time to perform research into all the latest trends and developments that affect your career?

Substance means having the character to make an investment in you truly worthwhile. The world has enough "empty suits" already! Do you only give your word when you are 100 percent committed and then follow it through at all costs? Do you always tell the truth, even when it hurts? Do you always maintain high ethics and personal honesty, eschewing the fast, cheap buck for hard-earned profits that will stay with you?

Follow the principles of MISS and you will surely hit your fresh target! After you have done all the groundwork, don't stumble on the execution!

TAKE YOUR PULSE: SELF-ASSESSMENT QUESTIONS MEASURING YOUR FRESHNESS EFFORTS

Now that you know all about what fresh really means and what it takes to achieve and maintain freshness in your daily professional and personal life, let's take your pulse and measure the health of your freshness efforts. Answer each question using the following scale of one to five hearts. Then add up the total and see how "heart-healthy" your level of fresh really is!

Scale

5 ♥♥♥♥♥	Strongly agree	That's really, really true about me.
4 ♥♥♥♥	Agree	That would be me.
3 ♥♥♥	Somewhat agree	50/50 sometimes, sometimes not.
2 ♥♥	Disagree	That absolutely has nothing to do with me.
1 ♥	Strongly disagree	Let me take the fifth on this.

What's Your Pulse Rate? 6.5 Questions Measuring How You Achieve Freshness

1. My friends and colleagues come to me for the most up-to-date information.

2. If you are looking for fresh ideas, I am the one.

3. My current skill set is the most competitive out of anyone I may come up against for a job and/or promotion.

4. I am aware of the latest technology that can help me personally and professionally.

5. When my friends and colleagues want a fresh perspective or strategy, I am the first person they call.

6. The last book I read was one that was published within the last 12 months.

6.5 My resume is current, up-to-date, and competitive.

Now that you've taken the test, let's analyze your score:

Scores

- **7–13:** Your freshness is expired. You know what that means: nobody wants to purchase your brand and you'll soon be taken off the shelf.
- **14–20:** Your freshness is day-old. There is minimal demand for your personal brand, but only at a steep discount and when the more popular and competitive brands are all sold out.
- **21–26:** Your freshness is canned. Your brand will sell if it stays on the shelf long enough, but anyone seeking real fresh results will look elsewhere.
- **27–33:** Your freshness is fresh frozen. Your brand is a respectable choice for the discerning connoisseur, but not the top choice.
- **34–35:** Your freshness is market fresh. Congratulations! You have the brand that is most in demand and fetches the highest prices. You sell out early in the morning, when only the most competitive shoppers are out evaluating the available brands.

IT'S SHOWTIME!: Develop the need to maintain freshness and take daily, weekly, monthly, quarterly, and yearly steps to put your plan into action

You have been given the 6.5 steps to achieving and maintaining freshness. Once you have followed them, it is time to take the extra step that will allow you to truly complete your quest for freshness. This step ingrains the need to constantly stay fresh into your everyday life on a permanent basis.

Remember, Fresh PASSION is not a quick fix, but a methodology for changing your approach to life so that you can achieve your maximum potential as a professional and as a human being. Use the chart that follows to track your continuing progress toward achieving and maintaining true freshness.

FREQUENCY	WHAT CAN I DO?	HOW DOES IT HELP MY BRAND?
DAILY	Regularly check the RSS feeds and email alerts you have selected to keep you informed about your area of brand expertise. Also be on constant lookout for new feeds to add.	RSS feeds and email alerts are the simplest and best way to stay current with the constantly changing flow of information about your area of brand expertise. Remember, information is power!
WEEKLY	Read a well-respected blog by an expert in your area of brand expertise.	Blogs are an important uncensored form of peer criticism and networking. You will often find out about the "real" happenings in blogs that more formal news sources will not mention.
MONTHLY	Attend a meeting of a professional association to which you belong. Actively participate: speak on issues, volunteer for committees and activities, run for elective positions. Also add one person to your network.	Associations are a great networking tool and provide an opportunity to gain valuable experience. For example, being treasurer of a group is valid financial management experience you can put on your resume!
QUARTERLY	Acquire a new professional skill you don't have. Also meet with three to five members of your network, either in person or virtually.	No matter how talented you are, today's employers expect you to be adaptable and to perform numerous tasks that may go beyond the scope of your job. Professional training and development is key to ensuring you have the skills to survive. Networking is one skill you must keep honed; unless you regularly stay in contact with your network, your networking skills will grow rusty and your network will erode along with them.
YEARLY	Evaluate and refresh your network.	Evaluating and refreshing your network allows you to prune members that no longer provide value, renew contact with members who can provide value, and it paves the way to add new members who bring previously unavailable value.

Text Message

If you can't say it succinctly, you can't say it at all. With these words of wisdom and all you have just learned in mind, write yourself a text message that sums up your strategy to keep your brand fresh in the space that follows. Write it like you would an actual text message—something you can read in 10 seconds or less. Poor spelling and smiley faces are strictly optional!

FRESH TECHNOLOGIES: iPODS & PODCASTING, SMARTPHONES AND TABLETS, INTERNET PHONE CALLS, WEB CONFERENCING

Staying fresh is really all about staying current. In the Information Age, staying current is easier said than done. Fortunately, there are numerous technologies available that can help you stay on top of constantly changing job markets, professional skills, and social networks. The iPod you use for listening to music can also be used for listening to podcasts—digital broadcasts of information specifically designed to be accessed via iPod. Podcasts are a great way to obtain valuable news and information "on the go"!

And of course, any on-the-go person knows about the endless variety of smartphones and tablet/portable computers that allow you to surf the Internet; send and receive emails and text messages; send and receive phone calls; store information; take photos; record video; and perform a whole host of other tasks anywhere you happen to be. I won't review the extensive list of mobile devices on the market, but be aware that technology companies are constantly releasing newer gadgets with more capabilities at lower prices. Research before you buy.

One interesting phenomenon that is gaining traction is the free or reduced-charge Internet-based phone call. A number of online services allow you to download software that enables you to place phone calls throughout North America and across the globe, for free or minimal costs. Skype is one of the best-known providers of free Web-based conference calls, and many other service providers offer low-cost or free phone calls using Voice-over-Internet Protocol (VoIP) technology. As with mobile devices, perform careful research before selecting or downloading any Internet telephone software.

Finally, maintaining a virtual network is easier with Web conferencing tools. This software allows users to collaborate, meet, present demonstrations, conduct training, and perform other group activities, all without leaving their computer. Web conferencing can bring far-flung members of a network together in real time in a way that closely mimics actual face-to-face interaction. Once again, research all your options before making any decisions.

BROWNIE BITE

I provide a free bi-monthly e-newsletter packed full of ideas, advice, and motivational messages, as well as special deals and discounts on a variety of products that can help you reach your aspiration. Visit http://www.MyFreshBrand.com to sign up today!

THE DOGGIE BAG: THE ACHIEVING FRESHNESS TAKEAWAYS

1. Without a fresh approach to your brand and your life, the PASSION methodology will not work. You can't just create your new personal brand today, put it on a shelf, and expect it to carry you throughout your professional career while you sit back and reap its rewards. Staying fresh means constantly building on your successes and upgrading your skills and abilities to remain current with the changing needs of the marketplace.

2. Freshness lurks everywhere. Your "fresh antennae" must be attuned to detect freshness where your competitors ignore it. Never assume that a person, place, or experience does not hold a valuable lesson you can apply to enhance your brand and your position in the marketplace.

3. Networking is one of the single most critical weapons in your freshness arsenal. The vast majority of today's hires are made through networking, and valuable peer information that you won't find in any official source is passed through networks. In addition to meeting people, successful networking requires extensive follow up and relationship building to breathe life into your network, which will otherwise quickly grow stale and useless.

4. Use modeling to help yourself stay fresh. Identify and research the most successful people in your area of brand expertise. They didn't get that way by accident, and probably learned many of their methods of success from role models of their own. Don't be afraid to strike out on your own path, but be open to appreciating the experience of those who have gone before you.

5. To help radiate freshness to the world around you, remember the acronym MISS (mindset, image, skills, substance). To truly achieve freshness, you must believe in your own fresh capabilities, display a fresh image in how you look and act, maintain a set of fresh skills, and possess fresh substance of character. Without these ingredients, your "fresh stew" will grow stale and cold.

6. Fresh PASSION is not a quick fix, but a methodology for changing your approach to life so that you can achieve your maximum potential as a professional and as a human being. Don't make the mistake of trying to achieve freshness all at once. Becoming fresh is a lifelong process that requires a dedication to constant improvement, growth, and maturation.

6.5 To ingrain freshness in your life, make sure you take steps toward freshness in your daily, weekly, monthly, quarterly, and yearly activities. Take both a short-term and a long-term view of freshness, and you'll never lose sight of it.

3

Fresh Passion: Preparing Yourself

Quotable Notable: Robert Baden-Powell

Brownie Point: No Matter How Good You Think You Are, You Can Always Be Better

Preparation—The Concept, Rationale, and Importance

6.5 Fresh Steps toward Preparing Yourself

- **Preparing Yourself: Step 1**—Determine what it is that you really want to do.
- **Preparing Yourself: Step 2**—Ask yourself: "Do I really want success?"
- **Preparing Yourself: Step 3**—Ask yourself: "What does personal and professional success look like?"
- **Preparing Yourself: Step 4**—Go the extra mile to push yourself.
- **Preparing Yourself: Step 5**—Determine how you will celebrate success.
- **Preparing Yourself: Step 6**—Determine who will help you on this journey to success and beyond.
- **Preparing Yourself: Step 6.5**—Make it Real and Keep it Fresh—Keep success flowing in.

Take Your Pulse: Self-assessment questions measuring your efforts to prepare yourself

It's Showtime!: Know that preparation is a lifelong commitment and take daily, weekly, monthly, quarterly, and yearly steps to put your plan into action

Fresh Technologies: Personal Organizers, GPS systems

Brownie Bite

The Doggie Bag: The Preparing Yourself Takeaways

> *"Be Prepared . . . the meaning of the motto is that a scout must prepare himself by previous thinking out and practicing how to act on any accident or emergency so that he is never taken by surprise."*
>
> —ROBERT BADEN-POWELL (1857–1941)

QUOTABLE NOTABLE: ROBERT BADEN-POWELL

A British military officer and baron, Robert Baden-Powell founded the World Scouting Movement, known in the United States as the Boy Scouts and Girl Scouts. Inspired by the bravery and dedication of young cadets he served with during the turn-of-the-century Boer War in South Africa, Baden-Powell hoped that Scouting would promote honesty, service, courage, citizenship, character, leadership, and health among young people. He successfully built a brand that today spans the globe and is universally recognized as helping to develop future leaders.

BROWNIE POINT: NO MATTER HOW GOOD YOU THINK YOU ARE, YOU CAN ALWAYS BE BETTER

After spending a couple of years at that first post-college job, I realized my situation had become stagnant and I was looking for a new job where I could grow personally and professionally. I wanted to stay within retail, because I enjoyed managing and leading people. I also knew I wanted to work for a larger company, one that could offer more opportunity for growth.

I got a call from a college buddy one afternoon, telling me that he had seen an ad in the paper for a retail manager opening at a Fortune 5 company, and that they would be interviewing the following week. I immediately located the ad and called the company's recruiter, who had me fax over my resume.

Two days later, the recruiter called back to schedule my first phone interview. During this initial conversation, the recruiter stressed that they were not looking to simply fill a role that day, but were looking for future senior leaders, people who could get results and lead other people as they grew into senior leadership. She went on to state that the chosen fast-track candidate would have to start out working in one of their stores to get a grasp of the business and to be more closely evaluated. I completed the 2.5-hour phone interview and quickly moved on to a second 2.5-hour phone interview with the recruiting manager, who essentially stressed the same things. They wanted to find someone with strong leadership skills who could get results through people.

Two weeks later, I had my third interview, a face-to-face sit-down at the company's offices in West Palm Beach, Florida (did I mention the job would "force" me to relocate to West Palm Beach?). I went through a panel interview with four executives from the company. I was told that they had narrowed the field down to seven candidates (of course I was one of them). I told them about my successes in my existing job as well as the successful leadership I had demonstrated in college, and explained how I would take what I had learned and apply it to my role as field retail manager to take the business to the next level.

The company extended an offer to me a couple of weeks later, so I moved to West Palm Beach and started out as the retail manager of a 24-hour convenience business, the type of business with the highest turnover in the high-turnover retail industry. I viewed it as a giant foot in the door of a Fortune 5 company, and learned during my first 90 days that I didn't want to stay in that particular position for too long. It was too much of a taste of reality.

I asked myself, "How do I get where I want to be?" I started eyeing a regional operational manager position (a senior leadership role in the company), which they had sold me on during the initial interview. They had promised if I performed exceptionally well here that the fast-track program I was a part of would allow me to accelerate my growth and move into a leadership role quickly. "If I want to get to that level, then this is my introduction to them and their introduction to me," I told myself.

So I obtained the description of the regional operational manager position and saw that its key attributes were the ability to lead different levels of people, influence others, drive deeper results, and generally maintain a competitive edge. I didn't want to waste any time on launching my journey to this senior leadership role. I decided it was time to begin networking with people who would help me more fully develop those skills so I could make sure my results stood out above my peers.

As a first step, I asked my boss, "What defines success for you? How do you rank the members of your team?"

He replied, "I most highly rank people who get results through people without being abrasive, who are concerned with development of others, who focus on delivering to the internal and external customer. Good team players."

This helped me identify my gaps that would possibly prevent me from running up the corporate ladder. My results were good, and I received high praise for customer service and motivating people, but I was number three out of the company's retail managers—two people were better. They were good team players that had reached out to others in the company. I, on the other hand, had been more selfish in my approach and focused on delivering results in my own little bubble.

I realized I needed passionate experts to work for me, but how would I motivate people to deliver above and beyond, and invest in their development so that they would invest in mine? I networked with peers and with executives above me; I called and emailed them asking to spend time and find out what they did. In return, I showed them how I performed exemplary customer service and motivated front liners to do the same—areas where I was superior to most managers in the company.

Furthermore, I noticed that the two retail managers ranked above me were outgoing people who were leading extra projects and generally going beyond the job and outside of their comfort zone. I signed up for a mentorship program for new managers and developed a new manager's survival guide (the company started using this as part of the field training for new managers). I also led a project on diversity and inclusion and how it impacted marketing and sales in the twenty-first century. Anything I could volunteer for, I did. Within 18 months, I was considered the number-one retail manager in the company.

PREPARATION—THE CONCEPT, RATIONALE, AND IMPORTANCE

Preparation helps you get a large part of the substance for your brand building. Earlier in your career, this can be used to help you conduct stellar interviews with the best companies and have your pick of the job that best suits your personal and professional goals. Later in your career, you can use preparation to make you a top performer and to obtain the promotions and accolades that will propel your career forward at a breakneck speed, while helping you attain a high level of personal and professional success.

Being prepared means continuing your education through classes, professional development, building and contributing to formal and informal networks, and simply maintaining an active intellectual interest and knowledge capital in your career and your life, staying current on the latest business trends and demands in your field, taking on project assignments, asking your boss what you can do to become a better performer, and seizing every opportunity to stay front and center by volunteering for committees and gladly accepting additional work.

Let's get this clear: *YOU* are solely and ultimately responsible for your personal and professional success, which is achieved by becoming a fresh and competitive brand and avoiding "generic" like the plague. You should ask your bosses, friends, Branding Board of Advisers (more on that shortly), and colleagues to do one or more of the following:

- Help enable your success.
- Assist in facilitating your success.
- Support your success.
- Enhance your brand and make it the most competitive on the market.

You want to build a brand that competes internally and externally in the open marketplace. The more universal appeal it has, the more competitive it is. You always want to increase the equity of your brand by staying fresh, thus increasing your competitive edge. This gives you an enormous amount of personal and professional freedom, which leads to greater personal and professional success. Remember this simple formula:

Brand Equity + Brand Freedom = Greater Success

When you become a competitive brand, you become a magnet for attractive opportunities internally and externally; you move to a phase where you are not sitting on edge if the company or organization announces some type of reorganization, right sizing, left sizing, middle sizing, downsizing, or going-out-of-business sizing. Nor will you get lost in a sea of generic resumes, and, for you entrepreneurs, you will spend less money and time trying to convince customers that you and/or your products and services are the "best." Instead, you will spend that time adding more value for the customer and offering an experience that they will knock your doors down to get to.

All this time and effort you are putting into preparation really comes down to laying the groundwork so you can achieve one direct goal: *Create brand demand so people pay you exponentially*. When you see the end result put so plainly, doesn't all the exertion suddenly seem much more worthwhile?

6.5 FRESH STEPS TOWARD PREPARING YOURSELF

While it may seem a little ironic to take 6.5 steps of preparation to become prepared, the reality is that everything in life, even preparation, takes preparation to achieve. Now say that three times fast! In all seriousness, true preparation is an orderly, logical process that I have broken down into 6.5 concise steps:

- *Preparing Yourself: Step 1*
  Determine what it is that you really want to do.
- *Preparing Yourself: Step 2*
  Ask yourself: "Do I really want success?"

- *Preparing Yourself: Step 3*
  Ask yourself: "What does personal and professional success look like?"
- *Preparing Yourself: Step 4*
  Go the extra mile to push yourself.
- *Preparing Yourself: Step 5*
  Determine how you will celebrate success.
- *Preparing Yourself: Step 6*
  Determine who will help you on this journey to success and beyond.
- *Preparing Yourself: Step 6.5*
  Make it Real and Keep it Fresh—Keep success flowing in.

Follow these steps and you will be surprised by not only how prepared you find yourself for any eventuality, but how much developing this kind of thorough preparedness will add value to your brand.

Preparing Yourself: Step 1—Determine what it is that you really want to do

This step may seem deceptively easy to follow. For most people, what you really want to do is "succeed." If pressed further, people will usually define success along the lines of "make lots of money" or "marry the girl/guy of my dreams" or even the catchall "be happy."

Money, love, and happiness are all worthwhile life achievements, but in and of themselves they represent abstract goals. How will you make lots of money? How will you land a professional career that equals success to you? What will you do to improve yourself personally so that you can attract your ideal mate? What will bring you true, lasting happiness? You've got to be more specific in defining what you want to do, because there is no way to truly prepare yourself to meet vague, general goals.

Let's take a more specific example from my own experience. An executive leader colleague once asked me the question and my response went something like, "I want a career that will allow me to lead a diverse team while progressively learning how to influence through deeper layers of a Fortune 100 organization. I also want to simultaneously build a personal brand that can compete internally and externally and help me achieve both personal and professional success."

Now, the end result of my achieving these specific goals may well wind up fulfilling more general goals of money, love, and happiness. If I become a leader at a Fortune 100 corporation, I will probably earn a big salary; success in the business world often makes people more confident and assertive, which are traits that a romantic partner will likely find appealing; and doing exactly what I want with my life should create feelings of self-worth and satisfaction that are key to any lasting personal happiness. If I hadn't taken the time to do some reflecting and determined what it is I really want to do, those general goals that almost everyone has would probably stay beyond my reach.

Preparing Yourself: Step 2—Ask yourself: "Do I really want success?"

This is another question whose answer is a lot less obvious than it appears at first glance. I hope you answered with a resounding "YES!" I know I sure did. But as with Step 1, really wanting concrete success is a different proposition than desiring success in the more general sense.

Really wanting concrete success means dedicating your entire life to doing what you really want to do and building your personal brand. It means making large personal sacrifices—you may have to move far from family and friends to take a key promotion, or volunteer to work extra time on the weekend, or take professional development courses on top of your already busy work schedule.

If you really want success, you'll make these types of sacrifices, and you may have to make them over and over. I'm not advocating becoming a workaholic to the point where you leave a spouse or child neglected, abandon other important family obligations, or become a complete recluse. I am, however, letting you know that really wanting success means making some hard choices and choosing long-term results over short-term pleasures.

If you're not willing to make these kinds of sacrifices, you may not really want the type of success this book is priming you to achieve. This book is preparing you to catapult yourself into exponential and sustainable success, not the common generic pseudo-success that only happens for a day or, at best, a season. You will by no means be doomed to a life in the gutter, but you will also likely find yourself stuck somewhere in the middle, looking up at the people who have built truly successful brands, quite possibly wondering why they got all the "luck" and you were left behind.

Preparing Yourself: Step 3—Ask yourself: "What does personal and professional success look like?"

This is one of those questions with no right answer. As mentioned earlier in the book, no two people will have the same notion of personal and professional success, nor should they. A salesperson seeking to climb to the top of his field has a very different end goal than a doctor seeking to climb to the top of her field. Likewise, someone who has always dreamed of a traditional home and family life has different personal priorities than someone who seeks the "single" lifestyle.

For me, success looks like having the financial ability to support a "beyond comfortable" lifestyle while giving financially, spiritually, and professionally out of my abundance of skills, talents, abilities, and assets. I want the recipients of my giving to be my friends, family, colleagues, and even strangers. Everything I do is geared toward helping to paint this picture of success.

For example, through this book I intend to share my skills, abilities, and assets with the reading public—which includes friends, family, colleagues, and strangers. Don't feel constrained by the boundaries of my picture of personal and professional success—paint your own. As long as it is an honest picture, it will never steer you wrong!

Preparing Yourself: Step 4—Go the extra mile to push yourself

I alluded to this step in Step 2. A big part of really wanting success is going the extra mile to push yourself. Notice I did not say "being willing" to go the extra mile, but actually "going" the extra mile. Our society heavily focuses on having the will to accomplish things, and it's true that without a strong will, no great achievements are possible. But just having the will without taking the action is like being a wallflower at the high school dance—you spend the evening gazing longingly at all the pretty girls you want to dance with and never ask any of them to dance!

So go the extra mile. Start now. Ask your company's HR department for a list of all open positions that are available above yours. If you see one that is a good fit with your personal vision of success, start doing whatever is necessary to make yourself a leading candidate. Extend your network and bring people in who can bring value to your personal and professional life. Do something that adds value for your customers that your competitors wouldn't think of doing. Spend 40 percent of your monthly time developing skills that will translate to the professional marketplace—these are just a few things you can do now.

Going the extra mile should never involve doing anything a person of reasonable conscience would consider immoral, unethical, or illegal. There are many dark and nasty shortcuts that may aid your rise in the professional world, but cheaters are invariably discovered, and the old adage that you see the same people on the way down as you did on the way up has stuck around so long because it is absolutely true!

Preparing Yourself: Step 5—Determine how you will celebrate success

Humans have an intrinsic need to celebrate successes. That is why we use rituals to mark victorious occasions. College graduations are noted with commencement ceremonies, weddings may be honored with both religious and secular festivities, and athletic achievements are rewarded with the public dispersal of medals and trophies.

Therefore, part of your preparation for building a brand that will deliver personal and professional success should be planning ways to celebrate your success. Keep in mind that the ritual does not have to mark the end of your celebration. Perhaps once you obtain a senior executive position in your field, you will want to have a party with family and friends. But what about the morning after? Successful college graduates, married couples, and athletes do not simply shut down after they celebrate their achievements. They move forward through their lives, continuing to find positive ways to make something out of the success they have achieved and seeking to maintain it at a high level.

In my case, I celebrate the success I have achieved by traveling the country and inspiring, motivating, and showing others how to achieve personal and professional success. I also plan to start a foundation where I can sow seeds into the lives of young people, especially in the area of personal branding and communication, and to spend six weeks a year visiting the world.

You may have very different notions about how to celebrate your success, and that is fine. Just remember that success is meant to be shared, not hoarded, and to those whom much is given, much is expected!

Preparing Yourself: Step 6—Determine who will help you on this journey to success and beyond

Overnight success is virtually impossible, and even in "self-made" success stories, individuals rarely do it entirely by themselves. A crucial part of the time and effort you need to put into building your successful brand is identifying and recruiting the people who will help you make it happen. I like to refer to this group of people as your "Branding Board of Advisers." I have my own board that I call the "Fresh Brown Board." This board is critical to my success.

Here are a few helpful hints on how to choose your own Branding Board of Advisers:

- Be willing to sow into personal and professional success; be willing to give more to them than they give to you!
- Seek out branded experts, especially ones who have achieved success in the area(s) in which you are aspiring to compete.
- Make sure they are smarter than you; if you are always the smartest person you are not feeding your success, you are feeding your ego and going nowhere.
- Get a commitment from them—ask them if they can be passionate about your success, believe in you, understand your brand, and be willing to give unselfishly.

- Ask them what you can do for them in exchange for their commitment. This is possibly the most crucial building block for your board. And don't just ask; have a genuine willingness to provide an equal commitment to anyone who joins your board. Remember that success is meant to be shared, and also that users, like cheaters, are always found out sooner or later (usually sooner).
- Make sure you pick the right experts—don't be afraid to rotate members off the board, especially when you feel like you are not staying fresh and growing personally and professionally.

Still a little unclear on what exactly constitutes a Branding Board of Advisers? Here are my actual positions on the Fresh Brown Board:

Chief Results Officer—That's me, Michael D. Brown. I am very clear that I own my success; although others might be facilitators, cheerleaders, and enablers—the buck stops here. If I fail or achieve less than my desired goal, it is ultimately my responsibility.

Finance Minister—He's my financial adviser who makes sure that I am on track with my success plan. I often think about voting him off, usually in April when he advises (he preaches, actually) me that I need to have a little more discipline with spending.

Keep It Real and Balanced Coach—She has been around the longest and has a candid way of reeling me in.

Director of Praise and Public Relations (four positions)—One person focuses on my work as a speaker, one focuses on my work as a coach, one focuses on my work as an author, and one focuses on my work as a trainer. They believe strongly in both my personal and professional brand, and they proactively spread the word. These folks also provide me with fresh feedback about what I can do to better meet the needs of new and future clients or employers.

Director of Brand and Creative Director—He makes sure that the brand is represented in everything that has my name attached to it: my resume, my business cards, my postage stamps, my voicemail, my signature on my email, my Facebook page, my Twitter page, my networking profile, my website, my book layout, my everything. He makes sure that it all ties back to my brand of Fresh Results.

Director of Interpretation—Thank God for this position, otherwise you would be reading a series of dreams, just as they came out. Whether I am on a plane, at dinner, driving down the road, or sleeping—a plethora of ideas just seem to flourish. So I grab whatever I can find and just start writing. My Director of Interpretation (also known as my editor) helps me make sense of it all.

Preparing Yourself: Step 6.5—Make it Real and Keep it Fresh—Keep success flowing in

Resting on your laurel wreath is easy, but it also signifies the death of your personal brand. The professional world is full of former success stories that burned out or gave up: people who stopped trying and started coasting on past accomplishments. Some people are able to make a decent living doing just that, but this mindset goes against everything Fresh PASSION is about.

Fresh PASSION is about maximizing your talents and abilities every day of your life, to achieve continuing success at levels you may never have imagined were possible. It is not about establishing a definite finish line and then hanging back and laying low once you reach it! So stay hungry—actually, stay starving—and never let yourself get totally satisfied—especially with mediocrity.

As with achieving and maintaining freshness, the acronym MISS (mindset, image, skills, and substance) is highly relevant to achieving and maintaining preparation (see the previous chapter for a refresher on MISS if you need to). MISS is one of the best ways to take that extra half step of taking your preparation out into the real world and constantly building it to newer and greater heights.

TAKE YOUR PULSE—SELF-ASSESSMENT QUESTIONS MEASURING YOUR EFFORTS TO PREPARE YOURSELF

How prepared are you? Have you taken the necessary preparations in your personal and professional life to establish a brand that will guarantee your success? It's time for a heart check on your preparedness level. Answer each question using the following scale of one to five hearts. Then add up the total and see how "heart-healthy" your preparation really is!

Scale

5	♥♥♥♥♥	Strongly agree	That's really, really true about me.
4	♥♥♥♥	Agree	That would be me.
3	♥♥♥	Somewhat agree	50/50 sometimes, sometimes not.
2	♥♥	Disagree	That absolutely has nothing to do with me.
1	♥	Strongly disagree	Let me take the fifth on this.

What's Your Pulse Rate? 6.5 Questions Measuring How Prepared You Are

1. I have a fully realized ideal of personal and professional success around which I build all my preparatory efforts.

2. I have the utmost confidence that I am truly prepared to achieve success and have no doubts about my ability to overcome any obstacle, no matter how unpredictable.

3. I have mastered the specific skills necessary to achieve success by being a branded expert in my chosen field.

4. I have obtained the credentials (the proper degree, certifications, advanced training, etc.) necessary to achieve success by being a branded expert in my chosen field.

5. I feel a burning competitive desire that pushes me to always take additional steps toward being prepared rather than feel satisfied with my preparatory efforts.

6. I know the skill sets and the mental attitudes of three people who have achieved success in the area in which I want to succeed.

6.5 I gain a new competitive skill on at least a quarterly basis.

Now that you've taken the test, let's analyze your score:

Scores

- **7–13:** Your preparation is winging it. You haven't taken any real steps to prepare yourself for success and are relying on blind luck and last-second thinking to overcome whatever obstacles come your way.
- **14–20:** Your preparation is hasty. You have taken a few quick steps to get ready to succeed, but hurrying now will only make success take longer to arrive later.
- **21–26:** Your preparation is by the book. You have done all the obvious things it takes to prepare for success in your chosen field, but so have most of your competitors. Those who take extra steps and think outside the box in their preparation are the ones who will stand out.
- **27–33:** Your preparation is game ready. You have gone above and beyond the norm to prepare and are ready for some serious competition. But are you ready to win?
- **34–35:** Your preparation is Scoutworthy. Bully for you! You have taken the words of Robert Baden-Powell to heart and have thoroughly prepared yourself for all contingencies, including unknowns, and done the groundwork necessary to truly stand out from the rest of the competition. You are fit to fight.

IT'S SHOWTIME!: Know that preparation is a lifelong commitment and take daily, weekly, monthly, quarterly, and yearly steps to put your plan into action

So you have followed the 6.5 steps to achieving true preparation for building a successful personal brand. If you have truly followed them, you know that preparation is an ongoing, lifelong commitment, and you should never reach a point where you think you are totally prepared and it's time to sit back and enjoy the fruits of your labor. Enjoyment and relaxation are certainly allowed (and encouraged), but not to the point that you lose your fresh edge!

Use the form on the following pages to track your continuing efforts at achieving maximum preparation for the kind of personal and professional success you know you deserve. In the spirit of never being prepared enough, we have included a blank "Overachiever" column in this chart where you can jot down ideas that will help you get and stay prepared even beyond your success-minded colleagues who have read this book and are following its advice!

FREQUENCY	WHAT CAN I DO?	HOW DOES IT HELP MY BRAND?	OVERACHIEVER
DAILY	Stay informed about current events by reading a newspaper, listening to a radio news broadcast, and/or watching a major television news broadcast. You can do this easily by setting up an RSS feed, which is a Web feed format allowing you to have relevant content from blogs, news sites, and other online sources of information constantly streamed to your desktop.	Keeping up with general current events allows you to learn about larger trends, ideas, and happenings that may have direct or indirect relevance to your specific brand niche. You will also learn about what's going on in the broader economy to understand what obstacles are being faced and how your brand can help solve these obstacles. Also as an informed person you will be a more interesting conversationalist and have more success at networking.	
WEEKLY	Perform a MISS review—examine how effectively you are preparing the mindset, image, skills, and substance portions of your brand.	MISS is not a one-time gut check. It is a constant reevaluation of how your thought process, way you present yourself, skill set, and overall personal substance are helping or hindering your efforts at success. Weekly check-ups will ensure that if you slip in any one of these areas, you will catch it and can rectify the situation before it becomes dire.	

FREQUENCY	WHAT CAN I DO?	HOW DOES IT HELP MY BRAND?	OVERACHIEVER
MONTHLY	Perform a market check—review the latest job openings, success stories, failures, news, and events in your branded area of expertise. Also speak with one member of your Branding Board of Advisers. For example, a large part of my brand expertise is helping retailers achieve double-digit growth to their bottom line. So I follow a number of retail trade publications to stay abreast of the trends and strategies that are being employed by the competition.	The marketplace is moving faster than ever, thanks to the Internet and other technologies. Jobs open and are filled quickly, new people succeed in new ways while established people grow stale and fall by the wayside, and today's hot skill is tomorrow's useless bit of knowledge. Monthly market checks will help you ensure you are taking preparatory steps that match the current needs of the marketplace.	
QUARTERLY	Arrange a meeting of your Branding Board of Advisers, either virtually or in person.	By bringing your entire Branding Board of Advisers together for a frank quarterly discussion, you can discover where the different aspects of your preparation are in sync and where they may be out of joint. This also allows you to see where you can help your board members!	

FREQUENCY	WHAT CAN I DO?	HOW DOES IT HELP MY BRAND?	OVERACHIEVER
YEARLY	Thoroughly review everything you have done in the past year to prepare yourself for success. Make at least one major change to your efforts and identify one right move to build upon in the coming year. Also evaluate and refresh your Branding Board of Advisers.	Preparation is a critical component of your career performance, so like your overall career performance, it deserves an annual review. You will undoubtedly discover at least one area where a major change is in order and hopefully will identify at least one success you can expand on in future preparatory efforts. Like your larger network, your Branding Board of Advisers needs an annual fine-tuning to make sure every member is the best person possible to help you succeed in a particular area of your brand.	

Text Message

Test your preparedness by writing a text message in the space here that explains how you have prepared yourself to build a successful personal brand. If you are truly prepared, you should be able to quickly describe the major points of your strategy in text message format, meaning it can be read in 10 seconds or less. Take inspiration from the brevity of the Scout motto—"Be Prepared"!

_____

_____

FRESH TECHNOLOGIES—PERSONAL ORGANIZERS, GPS SYSTEMS

One of the biggest hallmarks of a successful person is punctuality. Successful people are rarely late, always on time, and usually early. Most smartphones and portable computers have personal organizer/automatic reminder capabilities. Also a GPS system is a worthwhile investment for your automobile. Arriving to places on time by car is tough enough with the realities of modern traffic; there is no need to throw getting lost into the mix of travel delays!

BROWNIE BITE

Visit www.MyFreshBrand.com for a wide variety of downloadable features that will help you achieve Fresh PASSION in your life and career. You can also access a helpful MISS chart at www.MyFreshBrand.com that will ease your efforts to maintain the highest levels of mindset, image, skills, and substance preparation possible.

THE DOGGIE BAG—THE PREPARING YOURSELF TAKEAWAYS

1. Preparation is a key building block for your successful personal

brand. It provides much of your brand substance and allows you to meet and overcome challenges in a direct, forthright manner. Preparation means constantly continuing your formal and informal education—which means efforts such as obtaining advanced degrees and professional development, as well as networking and socializing with peers and superiors who can help you take the next step in your career.

2. YOU are solely responsible for your brand's success (remember the brand is who YOU are), and YOU must be accountable for any and all preparations that make success possible. Failure is not the fault of your advisers, friends, mentors, peers, or employers—it is YOUR fault for not preparing thoroughly or properly. Asking for help is not enough, you must know what help to ask for, who to ask it from, and when to ask for it! If you choose to seek advice from the wrong source, the source is not to blame. Don't get nervous; by the time you finish this book, you will want to be prepared to take complete ownership of your personal and professional success.

3. Success breeds more success. Once you have built a successful brand, job offers, promotions, and exciting new opportunities will start coming your way without your even looking for them. The phrase "a stitch in time saves nine" applies here. The earlier you prepare your successful brand, the earlier more opportunities become available to you, which propels you up the corporate or entrepreneurial ladder more quickly—which in turn brings even more opportunities that may have never existed if you had waited to start preparing. Preparation needs to begin NOW, and your reading of this book is the greatest kick up to your preparation.

4. To thine own self, be true. William Shakespeare knew what he was talking (or writing) about! All the preparation in the world won't help if you don't know what you're preparing for, or if you are preparing for someone else's vision of success rather than your own. The first step toward preparedness is to fully examine

your own wants and needs and determine exactly what personal and professional success looks like for YOU and you alone. Now you have a target to aim for.

5. Make sure you want and are ready for success. "Fear of success" is a very real phenomenon. Many people secretly don't want to succeed because they don't feel worthy or capable of handling it. Others want to succeed in theory, but in practice don't have the drive or determination to make it happen. Do a real gut check. If for any reason you aren't willing or ready to do what it takes, maybe you should put your preparation aside for a while until you're really excited and ready for the end result.

6. A crucial component of your preparation for success is to create a top-notch Branding Board of Advisers. Each board member should possess a level of expertise that can directly assist you in your preparatory efforts and be willing to make a personal investment in seeing you reach and exceed your goals. Remember that one good turn deserves another; be equally willing to help your board members in their own personal quests for success.

6.5 Fresh PASSION is about maximizing your talents and abilities every day of your life in order to achieve continuing success at levels you may never have imagined were possible. Therefore, you will never be fully prepared. No matter how much groundwork you lay or how high you soar, there are always more advance steps to take and greater heights to reach. Keep a little hunger burning in your stomach and never assume you've "got it made!"

4

FRESH PASSION: ASPIRING TO REACH YOUR GOALS

Quotable Notable: Arnold Schwarzenegger

Brownie Point: Standing Out—When the Going Gets Tough, the Tough Stay Focused

Aspiration—The Concept, Rationale, and Importance

6.5 Fresh Steps toward Aspiring to Reach Your Goals

- **Aspiring to Reach Your Goals: Step 1**—Identify your aspiration for personal and professional success.
- **Aspiring to Reach Your Goals: Step 2**—Check your aspiration with your Branding Board of Advisers.
- **Aspiring to Reach Your Goals: Step 3**—Make sure you have the passion to make your aspiration come true.
- **Aspiring to Reach Your Goals: Step 4**—Make sure you have the skills to make your aspiration come true.
- **Aspiring to Reach Your Goals: Step 5**—Make sure you have the determination to make your aspiration come true.
- **Aspiring to Reach Your Goals: Step 6**—Connect your aspiration to your perfect day.
- **Aspiring to Reach Your Goals: Step 6.5**—Make it Real and Keep it Fresh—Write it down.

Take Your Pulse: Self-assessment questions measuring your efforts to define and reach your goals

It's Showtime!: Maintain and move beyond your aspiration, and then take daily, weekly, monthly, quarterly, and yearly steps to put your plan into action

Fresh Technologies: Use calendar software to create an Aspiration Calendar

Brownie Bite

The Doggie Bag: The Aspiring to Reach Your Goals Takeaways

> *"For me, life is continuously being hungry. The meaning of life is not simply to exist, to survive, but to move ahead, to go up, to achieve, to conquer."*
>
> —ARNOLD SCHWARZENEGGER

QUOTABLE NOTABLE: ARNOLD SCHWARZENEGGER

Since arriving in the United States from his native Austria as a virtually penniless 21-year-old, Arnold Schwarzenegger has embodied the notion of setting extremely high aspirations and reaching them better than anyone. Among the impressive aspirations Schwarzenegger has turned into reality are winning the Mr. Olympia international bodybuilding title (seven times), becoming an international movie star, earning a million dollars in various business and real estate ventures by age 30, and being elected as governor of California. Probably the only one of his significant aspirations Schwarzenegger has ever failed to achieve is being elected as president of the United States, which he is prohibited from doing as a foreign-born citizen! Schwarzenegger has built his brand as a global celebrity by setting concrete goals and using passion, skills, determination, brains, charisma, and a huge supply of self-confidence to achieve them.

> *"Aim at nothing and you are absolutely guaranteed to hit it!"*
>
> —MICHAEL D. BROWN

BROWNIE POINT: STANDING OUT—WHEN THE GOING GETS TOUGH, THE TOUGH STAY FOCUSED

Harkening back to the Fortune 5 management job I described earlier, I had become frustrated in that position. It was taking a physical and emotional toll on me and my financial status was in worse shape than anyone would have guessed.

My long-term aspiration in that company, to take on a senior regional operations management role that led a team of more than 1,000 people, began to diminish. I started sending my resume to everyone. I applied to openings for a cigarette salesperson, loan officer, and restaurant manager—roles that my resume and background didn't really support.

I was taking the wrong attitude toward my job search—rather than looking for a meaningful position that would help me continue working toward my aspiration of managing large groups of people, I was simply looking for anything that would pay more money than my existing job was paying me. This attitude, which did nothing to actually enhance my budding career, came through in my interviews.

Despite the lousy, shortsighted attitude, I got a few job offers—such as the tobacco sales representative job I had interviewed for. They were all lateral or downward moves. I carefully thought them over and honestly asked myself whether any of these roles would help me reach my long-term goal of leading people and a career that would yield both personal and professional success. The answer was a resounding NO.

From this soul-searching I got renewed energy and was able to calm down and refocus. I sharpened my aspiration and the focus I had on my existing job. I finally realized that a wild goose chase for any new job someone dangled in front of my nose wouldn't help me obtain the broader leadership role I truly desired.

Before I could move on to this type of leadership position, I first needed to ensure that all supporting processes and roles were in place. For example, I needed to express my desire for advancement to my existing boss. I had never taken this step because I erroneously assumed he would simply know that I sought advancement. I also focused on the in-between roles that would lay the foundation and track record for the kind of success I would have to demonstrate before senior management seriously considered promoting me.

It was a focused and disciplined process, and I needed to prepare and motivate myself mentally. I knew that the job I wanted would involve a lot of traveling, so I occasionally went to the airport and watched planes take off, telling myself, "Soon, that will be a part of your life."

On Sundays, I'd visit open houses at nice homes to better understand the impact of a promotion—being able to purchase a bigger home. I invested in a wardrobe that would enhance the image of a senior leader. And since job interviews get harder as you move up the management chain, I started performing numerous mock interviews.

Furthermore, since I knew advancement would involve relocations (there ended up being seven in all), I studied different areas of the country where I might wind up living. All of this preparation gave me hope to hold on to and made the dream real. Crystallizing my aspiration through these activities allowed me to stay focused and understand the journey. There are things you absolutely need to make any aspiration come true—*passion, skills, and determination.* If I wanted to make my aspiration of leading people happen, I needed to go through the corporate "war zone" first.

ASPIRATION—THE CONCEPT, RATIONALE, AND IMPORTANCE

Aspiration means having particular ambitions and then setting out to achieve your goals. This is your purpose, to fly high and soar to greater heights! Knowing your aspiration allows you to tailor-build your personal brand; otherwise you run the risk of building a brand that doesn't help you reach your aspiration, which is a huge waste of time and resources.

What is your destiny? Is it to obtain a big promotion, start a successful business, receive awards and acclaim from your peers? Find your purpose(s), and no matter what they may be, put them on paper and post them everywhere—in the bathroom, in your car, in your journal—to serve as a reminder of what you are aspiring to do. The closer your aspiration aligns with your passion, the greater your chances for sustainable success!

6.5 FRESH STEPS TOWARD ASPIRING TO REACH YOUR GOALS

Aspiration, as defined in this book, is really a two-part entity: it is something that must be found and then realized. Many people have an aspiration, but relatively few genuinely *find* an aspiration that truly represents everything in life that they are most passionate about. Even fewer move on to *achieve* an aspiration once they have found it! The Fresh PASSION methodology is all about achievement, and by following the 6.5 steps outlined next, you can fully achieve your aspiration and thus live a richer, healthier, and more rewarding life that will yield personal and professional success.

- *Aspiring to Reach Your Goals: Step 1*
  Identify your aspiration for personal and professional success.
- *Aspiring to Reach Your Goals: Step 2*
  Check your aspiration with your Branding Board of Advisers.
- *Aspiring to Reach Your Goals: Step 3*
  Make sure you have the passion to make your aspiration come true.
- *Aspiring to Reach Your Goals: Step 4*
  Make sure you have the skills to make your aspiration come true.
- *Aspiring to Reach Your Goals: Step 5*
  Make sure you have the determination to make your aspiration come true.
- *Aspiring to Reach Your Goals: Step 6*
  Connect your aspiration to your perfect day.
- *Aspiring to Reach Your Goals: Step 6.5*
  Make it Real and Keep it Fresh—Write it down.

Aspiring to Reach Your Goals: Step 1—Identify your aspiration for personal and professional success

What are you most passionate about? Do you want to help children, build homes, create artwork, or lead and motivate people? Whatever the answer to this question is, that is where your aspiration lies.

Put aside the all-too-common thoughts of getting a job that will pay you the most money possible. That thought process is shortsighted and will only lead you to feeling unhappy and unfulfilled. Think long-term instead of short-term, think career instead of job, and think where you will be in 20 years instead of where you will be tomorrow.

It's not always easy to think using these parameters, but they are the parameters of success. Arnold Schwarzenegger was already a successful bodybuilder and businessman by age 30. He could have easily decided that he had already achieved enough and given up on his efforts to succeed as a film actor and politician.

Instead, Arnold remained focused on his long-term aspirations and became, for a time, the biggest movie star in the world—and also served as the governor of our most populous state from 2003–2010! Think about the personal and professional fulfillment he would have missed had he remained a fairly anonymous retired bodybuilder and successful entrepreneur. Identify your aspiration, and don't be afraid to have "Schwarzenegger-sized" ambitions. Your biceps may never be as big as his, but your success can be!

Aspiring to Reach Your Goals: Step 2—Check your aspiration with your Branding Board of Advisers

This is a tough, but ultimately necessary, step. An aspiration is a deeply personal and sensitive thing. It takes a great deal of courage to admit your innermost goals and desires to outside people and give them permission to be critical. But to truly find your ultimate aspiration, you must do just that.

Since your brand is built around everything you aspire to be and to achieve, your Branding Board of Advisers needs to be intimately involved with the crafting and refinement of your aspiration. Unless they know exactly what your ultimate goals in life are, they cannot fully help you reach them.

Part of your board's advisory role is to give tough love where it's needed and tell the truth even when it hurts. The members of your Branding Board should know you well enough to be able to judge whether your aspiration is realistic and best reflects your strengths, interests, skills, determination, and passions. If you are shy and introverted by nature, then perhaps Hollywood stardom or a career in politics are not aspirations that you have much chance of achieving. But maybe a career in the sciences would be a better way for you to maximize your potential and enjoy the most personal and professional success you could ever imagine.

A final note on subjecting your aspiration to a Branding Board of Advisers review: if you are truly uncomfortable with any of your advisers hearing your innermost goals or feel they are not properly qualified to advise you on something so personal and sensitive, it is time to refresh your board! The people on your board should be people you can tell anything to, hear anything from, and have absolute trust in.

Aspiring to Reach Your Goals: Step 3—Make sure you have the passion to make your aspiration come true

Pursuing an aspiration you don't have passion for makes about as much sense as pursuing a romantic partner you don't have passion for. The odds of successfully realizing an aspiration for which you lack passion are about the same as the odds of successfully creating a relationship with a person for whom you lack passion!

Saying that achieving an aspiration requires passion may seem like common sense, but you'd be surprised how many people waste entire lifetimes chasing dreams that don't really excite them. They switch jobs just to earn a few thousand extra dollars or take a promotion that will carry them away from doing what they love. Trust me, money is never easy!

No matter what your chosen area of branded expertise, achieving success and earning a high salary will take a significant amount of time and effort. You can shorten that time curve by becoming a branded expert that is fresh and competitive (and guess what: the proven road map with clear directions is in the book that you are holding). Why make things tougher on yourself by expending this time and effort in a field that you find dull, tedious, or unfulfilling?

Aspiring to Reach Your Goals: Step 4—Make sure you have the skills to make your aspiration come true

Much like Step 3, this step may appear to be common sense at first glance, but you'd be surprised how many people stumble over it! We Americans live in the land of opportunity; we are a nation of dreamers, and we are lucky for it. However, we also all too often obtain a sense of entitlement from living in a country where the "streets are paved with gold."

There is a widespread assumption that in America, if you have a dream and work hard at it, you will be successful. Having a dream and working hard are key components of any success story, but they are not the only components. For example, many people dream of opening their own restaurant. They can serve food the way they like it to be served, hobnob with their customers, and work for themselves instead of somebody else.

Opening your own restaurant is a fine and noble aspiration. But 90 percent of new restaurants fail in the first year, and there is a good reason for that. Running a restaurant is an incredibly difficult task that requires an extensive set of specific skills. Beyond having to know the ins and outs of food preparation, you have to know how to provide exemplary customer service; how to handle highly perishable inventory; how to manage the finances of a small business; how to identify, recruit, and train talented people; and how to think on your feet in a business that is always full of unpredictable surprises. Having a love for good cuisine and access to your grandmother's priceless family recipes will not cut it!

If you don't have a background or acquire the necessary skills in restaurant management (prior to opening the doors because your customers won't have the patience or desire to watch you learn as you go), your aspiration of opening your own successful restaurant will be virtually doomed to fail, even if you have a genuine passion for it. You need to pick up the necessary business skills. Beyond taking some restaurant management courses at a local university, it's time to roll up your sleeves and get a restaurant job. You may even have to spend a few years learning all the different aspects of the trade. But by putting in the time and effort to develop the necessary skills, you will make your aspiration far more attainable.

Aspiring to Reach Your Goals: Step 5—Make sure you have the determination to make your aspiration come true

So you think you have the passion and the skills to make your aspiration come true. How about the determination? Some people confuse "passion" with "determination," but they are entirely distinct personal qualities. Passion is a love for something deep enough that it brings joy to your life. Determination is a mindset that you will do whatever it takes (within ethical and legal guidelines!) to achieve your goals, no matter how difficult or challenging it may be.

Many people have a genuine passion for music and may play an instrument for their own personal enjoyment, but few have the determination to turn that passion into a career as a professional musician, which is probably one of the most difficult and competitive fields in which to achieve success. No matter how much deep-seated love you may hold for your instrument (we'll assume for argument's sake you have the necessary natural talent!), without incredible mental resolve you will never last through the endless series of auditions, rejections, and low-paying gigs that even the world's most successful musicians had to endure at the beginning of their careers.

Most of us do not seek a career in music, but success in any field requires an immense amount of determination. Companies are far more selective in their hiring processes than ever before—and also quicker to downsize than ever before (more on that later!). The competition to obtain a good job and move up the ladder is fierce these days, regardless of your line of work. Even if you are passionate and skilled, you will likely have competition that is either just as, or even more, passionate and skilled. Determination will set you apart from the pack once you move to the front of it.

So once you have identified your aspiration, had it approved by your Branding Board, and ensured that you possess the necessary passion and skills—now it is time to check your determination. How badly do you want success? Unless you can honestly answer "very badly, indeed," all your passion and skills will not likely take you past the middle. The world is full of high school dropouts who are self-made millionaires and Ivy League graduates who are struggling to get by.

Determination makes the difference. Grow complacent, or assume that you have enough passion and skills to slide on through, and you will almost surely be disappointed.

Aspiring to Reach Your Goals: Step 6—Connect your aspiration to your perfect day

At the beginning of the book, you were asked to fill out a worksheet describing your perfect day, including your workday. How does it begin? Do you rise for work first thing in the morning, or is your start time a little more flexible? Do you report to an office, sit in front of your home PC in a pair of slippers, or is the great outdoors your place of business? Before you can design any worthwhile personal and professional success plan, you must first answer these and many other questions about how your ideal day on the job would proceed.

Assuming you have already completed this worksheet, now it's time to take your aspiration and connect it to your perfect day. Hopefully, your aspiration and your perfect day are already at least somewhat in line. If your aspiration is to become an emergency room doctor and your perfect day revolves around working in a calm, low-key atmosphere, you need to rethink either your aspiration or your perfect day!

However, if you have already done a little soul-searching about what sort of life you wish to lead and have been honest about your aspiration and your perfect day, then you will probably find they fit together fairly well. There will still probably be some gaps that you need to identify and rectify.

For example, your aspiration may be to program computers, and your perfect day may involve having a lot of contact with co-workers and outside clients. Typically, computer programmers spend a good deal of time working either alone or with a small group of other programmers. They almost never have contact with outside clients. Bringing together this aspiration and perfect day is not impossible, but it may require a little finagling and compromising on your part.

Perhaps you could seek a job as lead programmer, or a liaison between the programming and sales departments, to broaden your contact with fellow employees while remaining actively involved with programming. Or you could even go a step further and get into the sales or marketing department of a computer technology firm, having plenty of contact with outside clients while leveraging your in-depth knowledge of how computers operate to create accurate, concise promotional campaigns.

Aspiring to Reach Your Goals: Step 6.5—Make it Real and Keep it Fresh—Write it down

It is all too easy to get sidetracked from our aspirations in life. For whatever reason, human nature seems to favor focusing on trivial short-term distractions more than meaningful long-term goals and strategies. Far too many of us simply live day to day, checking off an endless series of relatively unimportant tasks, errands, and diversions while letting our dreams slip away.

But this is not the way it turns out for those of us who imbue our daily lives with Fresh PASSION! By following the preceding six steps, you should be in good shape to retain a steady focus on the long-term, important goals in your life (while not completely ignoring the day-to-day details, of course—you will still have time to brush your teeth and grab a meal!).

Just to make sure you don't slip up, the 6.5 Step that will take your aspiration into the real world is writing it down on paper and placing it everywhere, so that throughout the day you are constantly reminded of the greater goal you are working toward and ensuring that some part of your activities that day are bringing you closer to realizing your goal. You should have a written note containing your aspiration posted on your bathroom mirror, on your fridge, on the back of your door, on your car dashboard, on the side of your home PC monitor, and anywhere else you are likely to see it at least once a day. At the end of this chapter there are some worksheets handy for writing your aspiration down and posting it, and even a few extra copies for your Branding Board members!

As a result, you will never be able to truthfully say you "forgot" your aspiration or that you got so caught up in your daily life that it simply fell by the wayside. Writing your aspiration down and placing it visibly all around you ensures that it remains as much a part of your daily life as all the little trivialities that can so easily derail you.

TAKE YOUR PULSE: SELF-ASSESSMENT QUESTIONS MEASURING YOUR EFFORTS TO DEFINE AND REACH YOUR GOALS

Are you satisfied that you have truly identified your aspiration and taken the necessary steps to make it a reality? Take your pulse and see how far you've really come. Answer each question using the following scale of one to five hearts, and find out exactly how close you are to reaching your aspiration!

Scale

5	♥♥♥♥♥	Strongly agree	That's really, really true about me.
4	♥♥♥♥	Agree	That would be me.
3	♥♥♥	Somewhat agree	50/50 sometimes, sometimes not.
2	♥♥	Disagree	That absolutely has nothing to do with me.
1	♥	Strongly disagree	Let me take the fifth on this.

What's Your Pulse Rate? 6.5 Questions Measuring How You Define Your Aspiration

1. I have identified an aspiration that accurately reflects where I would like to take my career and my life.

2. My Branding Board of Advisers is aware of my aspiration and I have solicited their feedback.

3. My aspiration aligns with my perfect day and there are no significant gaps between the two.

4. I have the passion necessary to achieve my aspiration.

5. I have the skills necessary to achieve my aspiration.

6. I have the determination necessary to achieve my aspiration.

6.5 I have written my aspiration down in more than one place so I am constantly reminded of it.

Now that you've taken the test, let's analyze your score:

Scores

- **7–13:** Your aspiration is a pipe dream. You may have fantasies about having a great career or richly rewarding personal life, but have made no efforts to make them come true or even to see if they really represent what you want in life.
- **14–20:** Your aspiration is a distant hope. You probably have some firm idea of what you would like to accomplish, but aren't making a real attempt to go out and do it.
- **21–26:** Your aspiration is outside, looking in. You know what you want and have taken some basic steps to get it. Maybe you know someone important in the field. You're probably at the stage where you're "looking into" achieving your aspiration. And when you're looking into something, it usually means you have an outside vantage point.
- **27–33:** Your aspiration is a realistic goal. You have followed most or all of the 6.5 steps to achieving your aspiration and have a credible shot at making it happen someday. Remember there is a difference between going through the motions and putting your heart into something!
- **34–35:** Your aspiration is a reality. You have fully integrated your aspiration into all aspects of your life and have made it your number-one daily priority. You have probably not achieved it yet, but you are on a clear path and have already passed several key milestones. You understand that goals are there to be met and surpassed, not held as an ideal.

Even if you manage to achieve your aspiration, your work is not done. Maintaining that aspiration and moving beyond it will still take constant effort and dedication on your part—just ask any of the numerous once-successful people who have found themselves bankrupt—sometimes only a few short years after they had "made it!"

IT'S SHOWTIME!: MAINTAIN AND MOVE BEYOND YOUR ASPIRATION, AND THEN TAKE DAILY, WEEKLY, MONTHLY, QUARTERLY, AND YEARLY STEPS TO PUT YOUR PLAN INTO ACTION

As has been stressed in earlier chapters, Fresh PASSION is about continually striving to do your best and achieve more, and never sitting back and assuming your work is finished (hint: think of the word FRESH that we talk about throughout the book). With that in mind, use the form on the following chart to help make your aspiration for success an integral part of your daily life.

FREQUENCY	WHAT CAN I DO?	HOW DOES IT HELP MY BRAND?
DAILY	Read your aspiration notes that you have left around your home, vehicle, and workplace. Don't skip any of them or simply glance—actually *read* them.	Without daily attention, your aspiration reminder notes will simply become another piece of background clutter you ignore as you focus all your energies on fulfilling short-term minor goals. Force yourself to read each note every day, and take a little time to think about what your aspiration means. This will keep it fresh in your thoughts and make the notes worthwhile.
WEEKLY	Find an example of someone who made their aspiration come true in a newspaper, magazine, website, or television broadcast. Study how they identified their aspiration and made it happen.	People are making their aspirations come true all the time. By studying a new real-life example every week, you will refresh your passion and determination, and also gain new ideas that may help you in your own pursuits.
MONTHLY	Review your progress on reaching your aspiration with one member of your Branding Board of Advisers.	Submitting your aspiration for review by your Branding Board is a critical step, but you need to continually engage them in your aspiration to gain the maximum benefit. Discuss the things you are doing to reach your aspiration with a board member and solicit honest feedback and criticism—this will keep your efforts fresh and allow you to quickly identify and rectify errors and missteps on your part.

FREQUENCY	WHAT CAN I DO?	HOW DOES IT HELP MY BRAND?
QUARTERLY	Obtain one new skill that will help you reach your aspiration.	No matter how skilled you are, you can always expand your skill set in ways that will bring you even closer to your aspiration. This could involve taking a course, securing a meaningful job, undergoing on-the-job training, or even conducting personal research. The key is to keep your career skills fresh, updated, and vital.
YEARLY	Carefully review your stated vision of a perfect day and see if it still matches your ideal. Make any changes to your perfect day that are necessary to reflect your current state of mind and then alter your aspiration as needed to fill in any gaps.	Your idea of a perfect day will likely change as your life changes. What may seem ideal one year could seem trivial the next. A yearly review will help keep both your perfect day and your aspiration fresh and in line with your heart's true desires.

Text Message

Help turn your aspiration into reality by writing a text message in the space provided that details the goal you are aspiring to. Sum it up in text message format so that anyone can discover the nature of your aspiration in 10 seconds or less. If it's too convoluted to explain, it's probably too convoluted to achieve!

_____

_____

_____

FRESH TECHNOLOGIES: USE CALENDAR SOFTWARE TO CREATE AN ASPIRATION CALENDAR

There are a number of inexpensive software tools available that allow you to create your own calendar from the comfort of your desktop. Why not create your own personal yearly Aspiration Calendar, with specific reminders of your goals and the steps you must take to achieve them? There may be certain dates you want to highlight, such as the start of an important skill-building class or the anniversary of your hire (perfect time to ask for a raise and/or promotion!) You could also include some catchphrases and slogans to pump yourself up—you've probably bought calendars featuring the inspirational words of others, so why not include some of your own?

BROWNIE BITE

I provide a free bi-monthly e-newsletter packed full of ideas, advice, and motivational messages, as well as special deals and discounts on a variety of products that can help you reach your aspiration. Visit http://www.MyFreshBrand.com to sign up today!

THE DOGGIE BAG: THE ASPIRING TO REACH YOUR GOALS TAKEAWAYS

1. Before you can successfully pursue your aspiration, you must clearly identify exactly what you want to accomplish in your professional and personal life. If you don't identify your aspiration, you fall into the generic category, and we know this is a struggling category that does not yield the highest level of personal and professional success. So think beyond the simple things like having a high salary or vacation home. Do you want to lead people? Do you want to serve as a role model to young people? Do you want to be in a position to help your community?

   By fully fleshing out everything you want to accomplish with your life, you can narrow your aspiration down to something that will truly bring you happiness and keep you motivated to succeed through what will likely be a grueling process.

   Knowing your aspiration will allow you to tailor build your brand, otherwise you run the risk of building a brand that is not connected to your aspiration—this is dangerous.

2. In addition to identifying your aspiration, you need to identify your perfect day. How would the ideal workday proceed for you, starting when you wake up in the morning and ending when you go to bed at night? What kinds of people would you deal with? What would your work environment look like? How busy would you be? Would you be giving direction to lots of employees or pursuing solo projects? Once you know what your perfect day looks like, you need to compare it to your aspiration and then fill in any gaps that exist between the two. Unless your aspiration leads you to your perfect day, it probably needs a little fine-tuning.

3. Being "good" is not enough to reach your aspiration. Having high grades or exemplary work performance reviews is important, but an outstanding record on its own is no guarantee of success. You need to take the next step and actively promote yourself and engage with people who can help you reach your aspiration.

Volunteering for and taking leadership roles in clubs, committees, events, and social organizations is necessary to make yourself stand out from the many other "good" candidates out there so that you can join the "great" category!

4. You must remain focused on your aspiration, even when times get tough and it seems like a different path might be easier to follow. As you pursue your aspiration, there will likely be temptations to change your focus in order to take a higher-paying job in another field or to launch a business venture that requires a different type of expertise. These distractions may offer some relief from short-term difficulties, but in the long term, allowing yourself to be distracted will take you away from your aspiration and your chance for true happiness and personal and professional fulfillment. You are better off trying to improve your attitude, expand your network of contacts, develop new advisers for your Branding Board, or even change your immediate circumstances while remaining on the path toward your ultimate aspiration.

5. Reaching your aspiration will take plenty of passion, skills, and determination. Passion means you aspire to do something you truly love, and not something you think will lead to wealth or an easy work schedule. Skills mean you have all the capabilities needed to make your aspiration come true, both the ones you learn and the ones you naturally possess. Determination means you have the tough, focused mindset necessary to fully commit yourself to achieving your aspiration, even when the odds are stacked against you.

6. Make sure your Branding Board of Advisers knows about your aspiration and has a chance to weigh in and offer constructive feedback. These should be the people whose judgment you value the most and in whom you have absolute trust. If you feel uncomfortable letting them evaluate your personal goals and dreams, you probably need new board members!

6.5 Keep your aspiration as an active part of your daily life. It is not a mission statement, best-case scenario, or fantasy. It is your life's goal that you are constantly striving to achieve through everything you do! Surround yourself with written reminders of your aspiration, read about the experiences of others who have reached their aspiration, discuss your aspiration regularly with your Branding Board, friends, family, and co-workers. Remember, a dream is useless if you don't wake up and realize it!

MY ASPIRATION WORKSHEET

In the space below, write out your aspiration. Go into detail if necessary—describe exactly what you would like to do with your career and your personal life. Then post copies of this worksheet in places where you will see it every day and also provide copies to your Branding Board of Advisers, friends, family, co-workers, managers, and anyone else who can help you realize your dreams.

_____

_____

_____

_____

_____

_____

_____

_____

_____

_____

_____

Please visit www.MyFreshBrand.com for more worksheets to share your aspiration with others.

5

Fresh Passion: Staying Laser-Focused

Quotable Notable: Bill Cosby

Brownie Point: "They'd Be Crazy to Get Rid of You"

Staying Laser-Focused—The Concept, Rationale, and Importance

6.5 Fresh Steps toward Staying Laser-Focused

- **Staying Laser-Focused: Step 1**—Start with the end in mind.
- **Staying Laser-Focused: Step 2**—Look at your aspiration and commit to making it your main focus.
- **Staying Laser-Focused: Step 3**—Share your commitment to focus on your aspiration with friends, family, colleagues, and Branding Board members, and ask for their help in maintaining it.
- **Staying Laser-Focused: Step 4**—Start each day by reviewing a focus list.
- **Staying Laser-Focused: Step 5**—Practice a "swift kick" to use on yourself when your vision begins to blur due to competing things or agendas.
- **Staying Laser-Focused: Step 6**—Create a "focus sanctuary."
- **Staying Laser-Focused: Step 6.5**—Schedule a conference call with yourself.

Take Your Pulse: Put your finger on the pulse of your focus efforts

It's Showtime!: Commit to remain focused throughout your life and take daily, weekly, monthly, quarterly, and yearly steps to put your plan into action

Fresh Technologies: Use financial management software to eliminate debt so you can maintain focus

Brownie Bite

The Doggie Bag: The Staying Laser-Focused Takeaways

> *"Anyone can dabble, but once you've made that commitment, your blood has that particular thing in it, and it's very hard for people to stop you."*
>
> —Bill Cosby

QUOTABLE NOTABLE: BILL COSBY

For fifty years, Bill Cosby has dedicated himself to providing intelligent, insightful comedy, and along the way he has become one of the most popular and successful entertainers of our time. Cosby broke historic TV racial barriers in the 1960s drama *I Spy*, 1970s animated series *Fat Albert and the Cosby Kids*, and 1980s sitcom *The Cosby Show*, and he remains a highly successful stand-up comic and has also appeared in many successful films. A U.S. Navy veteran, Cosby holds a PhD in education (earned in the 1970s when he was already a major show business celebrity!) and has been active in humanitarian causes for decades. Cosby's laser focus on the numerous ways he pursues his aspiration of entertaining people while helping them improve their lives is a perfect example to follow for anyone seeking success in any endeavor.

BROWNIE POINT: "THEY'D BE CRAZY TO GET RID OF YOU"

Over the years, I have built my personal brand to compete both internally and externally. I've had people at various jobs tell me, "They'd be crazy to get rid of you," and that's exactly how I want my superiors to think of me. Layoffs and firings may be unpleasant, but they are also a fact of life, and if you get too comfortable with your internal job situation, you expose yourself to a higher risk of falling victim to the next corporate downsizing. An experience I had early in my professional career perfectly illustrates the critical need to remain competitive among your peers at your job, as well as among your peers in the wider employment marketplace.

Two years into my corporate career at a Fortune 5 company, I was sitting in my office and got a call from a friend working at a different company. He relayed a rumor he had heard that my company was part of a major merger. Analysts were calling a buyout, and my multibillion-dollar global organization was being purchased!

All of my pride and passion for my company instantly welled up inside me and I started vehemently denying this rumor to my friend. Nobody was big enough to buy us! My friend patiently listened and then advised me to start sending my resume out anyway, since he had also heard my company would be cutting 10,000 jobs.

Despite all my confidence, I began thinking *What if?* I was new and had heard that when it came to layoffs, protocol usually dictated last in, first out. So I started calling other colleagues; it turned out they had all heard the same rumor, which I heard myself on NPR later that afternoon.

I faced a situation where my career might come to a halt; communications were scarce, senior management hadn't told us anything, and the whole rumor had spread through a leaked internal memo. As a side note, this was the first of eight mergers and reorganizations that I've now gone through. The names became fancier and more camouflaged over time—"downsizing," "outsourcing," and, my personal favorite, "business transformation."

I said to myself, "Stay focused on delivering here; if they let you go, they let you go." So I stayed focused on keeping my team together and delivering the same high-value services as always. All of this was in the face of general employee morale that couldn't have been lower. I'm not sure why I didn't internalize the negativity surrounding me, but I decided to do what I'd always done—that way senior management would have to honestly say that I was still delivering at a high level, so maybe they shouldn't let me go. After all, anyone who could deliver in this uncertain environment deserved to stay. I also wanted to be a good role model for my employees, as I still had the aspiration to take on larger teams and higher leadership roles.

I made it through the merger and subsequent round of layoffs unscathed. Every following year, a similar series of events took place. After the third merger, I noticed that I was often rewarded in the aftermath. I willingly relocated all across the country to take on new positions in the company and acquired a reputation as an agent of change, and as someone who delivered outstanding results with and through people in what might be politely called "uncertain and fragile" circumstances.

This skill became my brand: "Michael Brown can get it done and deliver outstanding results." I didn't know my brand had penetrated the organization as deeply as it had. People make the mistake during reorganizations (another great euphemism for "round of layoffs") of stopping work and losing focus. This behavior will be fresh in the minds of decision makers as they determine who stays and who goes. In times of uncertainty and change, you must deliver; you can do this while simultaneously focusing externally on opportunities that will enhance and grow your brand.

During the first merger I survived, I actively proved my value to my superiors as I was simultaneously preparing for a possible layoff by calling on my external network and letting them know I could potentially be out of a job and in need of recommendations. I was not calling this network my Branding Board yet, but it was the early version of the Branding Board I have been building since college, which uses two lenses: external and internal. The most important thing to remember about building a brand that can compete internally and externally is to keep the network fresh!

STAYING LASER-FOCUSED—THE CONCEPT, RATIONALE, AND IMPORTANCE

Laser focus is the key to every aspect of the Fresh PASSION formula. Without intently focusing on each one of these areas, you'll miss the mark and not deliver your brand. Life has a way of tempting us to lose focus and become disillusioned, so it is your responsibility to maintain your laser focus on building a foundation that is tailor-made for personal and professional success.

Let's think in military terms for a moment—the most firepower on the smallest target wins. A tiny laser burns through thick steel walls. You need to apply this same intense laser focus to the aspirations you've previously noted.

Let me give an example of the dangers of not staying laser-focused. A potential client wanted to have lunch with me to talk about how he could grow his struggling fitness business. I asked him what was causing his business to collapse, and he said he just couldn't get the customers to come back after their initial sessions. He said he was going to close that location and open up another location about 40 miles away. He went on to state that he was going to sign the lease in two weeks and that the new place was beautiful. What he really needed to do was focus on what was causing customers not to return rather than spending his time trying to open a new business that would likely fail as well.

No matter the distractions, no matter what comes your way, it is most critical that **you stay focused.** The ability to stay focused is often the difference between achieving your aspiration versus not achieving your aspiration.

6.5 FRESH STEPS TOWARD STAYING LASER-FOCUSED

- *Staying Laser-Focused: Step 1*
  Start with the end in mind.
- *Staying Laser-Focused: Step 2*
  Look at your aspiration and commit to making it your main focus.
- *Staying Laser-Focused: Step 3*
  Share your commitment to focus on your aspiration with friends, family, colleagues, and Branding Board members, and ask for their help in maintaining it.
- *Staying Laser-Focused: Step 4*
  Start each day by reviewing a focus list.
- *Staying Laser-Focused: Step 5*
  Practice a "swift kick" to use on yourself when your vision begins to blur due to competing things or agendas.

- *Staying Laser-Focused: Step 6*
  Create a "focus sanctuary."
- *Staying Laser-Focused: Step 6.5*
  Schedule a conference call with yourself.

Staying Laser-Focused: Step 1—Start with the end in mind

It's hard to maintain a laser focus without a concrete end goal on which to center your focus. You can stay laser-focused on a single target by using multiple lenses. For example, my ultimate professional goal has always been to motivate and lead large groups of people and achieve world-class results with and through people.

While staying laser-focused on that end goal, I have also aimed my focus through lenses such as remaining employed in times of reorganization, actively participating in volunteer activities and groups, keeping my skills fresh and competitive, and constantly building my network of professional contacts. All these other activities help me reach my end goal. They are not distractions but merely different aspects of what I'm trying to accomplish with my career and my life.

It is also important to always keep your ultimate aspiration in mind—achieving your perfect day. Etch your perfect day into your brain so that you are always thinking of it and tailoring your efforts to help you make it a reality. In addition, remember that you will never fully reach your end goal—there is no resting on your laurels with Fresh PASSION! If you honestly ever reach the point where you totally reach your aspiration and are living your perfect day, it's time to regroup and find ways to achieve even greater accomplishments and a more rewarding daily existence!

Staying Laser-Focused: Step 2—Look at your aspiration and commit to making it your main focus

This step may seem self-explanatory or redundant, but I include it for a very important reason. Even while intently pursuing your aspiration, it is astoundingly easy to get distracted or diverted to another path. You may be offered a great promotion or new job with better pay, working conditions, and professional prestige. But if taking it does not bring you closer to your aspiration, you must stay laser-focused and continue to seek out the offer that does make your aspiration that much closer to becoming reality.

When you do this, you will notice that you will be enhancing and making your brand more competitive in the process, which leads to you becoming that fresh and competitive branded expert who can realize exponential personal and professional success.

In contrast, "job-hopping" is a practice of constantly switching jobs or even careers, usually with making more money as the chief motivator. In this age of uncertain employment stability and instant gratification, job-hopping has become increasingly prevalent, and employers are even starting to take a softer view toward it, accepting the fact that many employees will simply not stay around for very long.

But job-hopping, unless you are hopping along a very clearly defined path that leads straight to your aspiration and the enhancement of your personal brand, is the antithesis of Fresh PASSION. I'm not recommending you blindly stay with an employer regardless of the company's circumstances or never try anything new. Stay competitive—internally and externally—by becoming a branded expert who continues to add equity to your brand by seeking out growth opportunities such as learning experiences, skill attainment, and education. If things are getting tough where you are, by all means look around for better opportunities, but don't jump out of the frying pan into the fire. Instead, jump into a pot of boiling opportunities (internally or externally) that will grow your personal brand and add equity. Also remember to take the opportunity to buckle down and do your best work while your peers wring their hands and complain. Believe me, you'll be noticed!

Staying Laser-Focused: Step 3—Share your commitment to focus on your aspiration with friends, family, colleagues, and Branding Board members, and ask for their help in maintaining it

"Going it alone" appeals to something in the American character—think of the silent, sturdy heroes played by legendary actors such as Clint Eastwood and John Wayne. Do you think Dirty Harry shared his aspirations to single-handedly rid San Francisco of criminals with his loved ones (if he even had any loved ones)?

Despite your natural desire to do things for yourself and avoid asking for help, accomplishing feats as monumental as achieving your aspiration and maximizing your personal and professional success is hard enough with assistance, never mind all by your lonesome! The whole point of building a broadly based network is that it can provide you with the support you need to maintain laser focus on your aspiration. But if the members of your network don't know what your aspiration is or of your commitment to focusing on it, then your network will fail you when you need it most.

Another positive side effect of letting all the important people in your life know about your aspiration and your laser focus is that you will have a much more difficult time slacking. Humans are curious by nature, and undoubtedly members of your network will regularly check in to see how you are progressing and whether they can offer any help. Humans are by nature also deathly afraid of embarrassment, and you will have extra motivation to remain laser-focused so that you have some results with which to back up your words. Even Dirty Harry always worked with a partner (although fans of the movies know how those partners typically ended up!).

Staying Laser-Focused: Step 4—Start each day by reviewing a focus list

When I say stay laser-focused, I'm not just throwing buzzwords around. Reaching your aspiration needs to be something you are constantly thinking about and acting on. A daily review of a list of goals, objectives, tasks, and responsibilities you need to fulfill to reach your aspiration will go a long way toward keeping your aspiration in the front of your mind.

Don't simply list a bunch of items like "get to work early" and "contact former manager for reference." Allot an ample amount of time to complete each item and include concrete steps and strategies for each one. What will you do to shave time off your morning routine to reach work early and what extra tasks will you accomplish once you get there?

How will you reach out to your former manager (phone call, email, office visit), and how will you frame your request?

Also, build in some break time (Even followers of the Fresh PASSION methodology are allowed to take a little time to have a sandwich or simply watch the sunset.) and a reasonable reward at the end of the day for your efforts. Your list should also include any carryover items that weren't completed the previous day—but not too many!

Staying Laser-Focused: Step 5—Practice a "swift kick" to use on yourself when your vision begins to blur due to competing things or agendas

We all know someone who could use a good swift kick to the posterior to clear their head of foolishness and set them straight. From time to time, that someone will be you. It has certainly been me!

No matter how dedicated, focused, talented, smart, creative, or generally awesome you are, you're still a person. And people make mistakes. There will be times when your vision blurs and your focus wanes because of distractions by things that seem important but really don't contribute to achieving your aspiration. These could include petty squabbles over corporate turf (I will delve more deeply into the murky waters of office politics in a later chapter.), an unintended minor slight or insult by a colleague, or even something as mundane as putting off important work to watch a favorite television show. (Buy a DVR or get on demand TV, folks!)

You need to be able to give yourself a swift kick when you recognize the symptoms of blurry vision. The kick could be a success mantra you repeat to yourself, a 15-minute jog to clear your head, a quick shower to cool off, or almost anything else that will pull you away from your distraction and snap you back into reality. Please remember that while the kick part is metaphorical, the swift part is very real. Taking a three-hour nap does not apply!

Staying Laser-Focused: Step 6—Create a "focus sanctuary"

If you follow the steps of Fresh PASSION, you will be a very busy person. You will often be surrounded by noise, activity, and general chaos. This is all necessary to achieve maximum success. But unchecked, all of that hubbub can lead to discouragement and burnout.

Sometimes we all need to step back and recharge our batteries a little bit. I'm not talking about a two-week Hawaiian vacation here, unfortunately, but about small activities you can take part in on a regular basis to give yourself a little peace and privacy to counterbalance your hectic life. Perhaps you have a favorite hobby, recreational activity, or sport you can take part in. Your focus sanctuary can also be a physical place, like a den in your home where you can relax on the couch. It can even be a task, like gardening.

Whatever your focus sanctuary is (and you can have as many as you want), it should be an activity or place that brings you peace of mind and allows you to simultaneously get away from your aspiration for a little while and refocus on it with a new, recharged attitude.

Staying Laser-Focused: Step 6.5—Schedule a conference call with yourself

You don't have to actually call yourself on the phone, although now that almost everyone has at least two phone numbers this would be fairly easy to do. What you need to do is work in some "me time" on a daily, weekly, and monthly basis.

Your conference call can be brief, but it should be meaningful. Have an internal dialogue with yourself (or talk to yourself out loud if you want, although I do not recommend doing it in public, especially not on an airplane!) about your aspiration and how effectively you are working toward achieving it. These "conversations" will likely bring to light otherwise missed observations and insights about things that are working and things that aren't. Flexibility is an important part of maintaining a laser focus on your aspiration. Maybe your aim is a little left or a little right of the target, and you need to make a few adjustments to get your bead back on the bull's-eye.

TAKE YOUR PULSE: PUT YOUR FINGER ON THE PULSE OF YOUR FOCUS EFFORTS

Have you locked in on your aspiration with a laser focus? Take the Heart Check to find out just how much intensity your focus really contains.

Scale

5	♥♥♥♥♥	Strongly agree	That's really, really true about me.
4	♥♥♥♥	Agree	That would be me.
3	♥♥♥	Somewhat agree	50/50 sometimes, sometimes not.
2	♥♥	Disagree	That absolutely has nothing to do with me.
1	♥	Strongly disagree	Let me take the fifth on this.

What's Your Pulse Rate? 6.5 Questions Measuring How You Stay Laser-Focused

1. I find myself occupied by multiple focuses that are related to each other and lead to a common goal.
2. It seems like I am constantly focusing on what it takes to succeed.
3. It is nearly impossible to persuade me to take my eyes off the prize.
4. I tend to focus on long-range goals and aspirations rather than mundane, trivial, and/or short-term concerns.
5. The people closest to me are aware of my focus on my aspirations.
6. I find that my focus is rarely blurred.

6.5 I avoid people and things that distract me.

Now that you've taken the test, let's analyze your score:

Scores

- **7–13:** Your focus is scattered. You allow yourself to be completely distracted from your goals and aspirations by petty and meaningless things, and probably haven't identified a primary aspiration. You will have virtually no chance of achieving true success in life until you buckle down and force yourself to focus on something concrete, meaningful, and long term.
- **14–20:** Your focus is unsteady. You may have identified a legitimate aspiration and are making some effort to achieve it, but you are too easily distracted to make much headway.
- **21–26:** Your focus is steady but dim. Your aspiration is in sight and in mind, but at a distance. Your focus is there, but not strong enough to make your aspiration a reality.
- **27–33:** Your focus is steady and clear. You think long term and consider your aspiration before making any major decision. But something is still missing—maybe your loved ones don't really know about your aspiration or you would be willing to change your path if the "right offer" came along.
- **34–35:** Your focus is laser-sharp. Excepting family and health, your aspiration is the single most important thing in your life. You are always working toward your aspiration in everything you do and you ignore or eliminate any distractions or temptations that pull you away from it.

Confused by how the scoring went this time? You either didn't read the introduction to this section or already forgot what you read. That means you lost focus while reading the book. Shame on you! Now go back to the beginning of the section and read it again. And for your punishment, no brownies after your supper tonight!

IT'S SHOWTIME!: Commit to remain focused throughout your life and take daily, weekly, monthly, quarterly, and yearly steps to put your plan into action

Maintaining laser focus on your aspiration over the course of your life is probably one of the most difficult parts of Fresh PASSION, but also one of the most necessary. You cannot pick and choose times to be laser-focused, because you never know when a distraction will pop up unannounced. Follow the chart on the next page to ensure that you remain laser-focused on a daily, weekly, monthly, quarterly, and yearly basis.

FREQUENCY	WHAT CAN I DO?	HOW DOES IT HELP MY BRAND?
DAILY	Review your daily focus list of goals, objectives, tasks, and responsibilities that must be met to keep you on the path toward your aspiration.	Maintaining and following a daily checklist keeps your mind sharp and your aspiration at the front of your thoughts. It is all too easy to have a "down day"; this will help you avoid having one!
WEEKLY	Visit your "focus sanctuary."	Your focus sanctuary is an activity, task, or place you can turn for peace and clarity. At least once a week you should take a little time to pursue a hobby or interest, or visit a favorite secluded spot, to clear your mind of stress and distractions so that you can refocus even stronger and sharper when you return.
MONTHLY	Conduct a focus review with a family member, colleague, or Branding Board member.	Beyond informing the important people in your life about your focus and aspiration, you should actively solicit feedback from them. Conduct a monthly "focus review" where one of these people provides honest input and criticism of how well you are maintaining your focus and minimizing distractions. Use this feedback to make any needed changes or improvements in your focus approach.

FREQUENCY	WHAT CAN I DO?	HOW DOES IT HELP MY BRAND?
QUARTERLY	Identify and eliminate one major distraction.	Ignoring distractions is easier than eliminating them, but at least once per quarter you should permanently remove one distraction from your life. This could mean ending contact with someone who is a bad influence, leaving a job that is not helping you reach your aspiration, or ceasing an extracurricular activity that does not relate to your aspiration.
YEARLY	Have a conference call with yourself.	At the very minimum, you should have an annual conference call with yourself where you schedule some "me time" to mentally review your aspiration and the things you do to stay laser-focused on it. Don't be afraid to make some changes based on this "conversation"!

Text Message

Stay laser-focused on your aspiration by writing a text message that describes how your aspiration remains at the center of your thoughts in the space here. Laser focus is intense and narrow, so you should be able to capture its essence in a message that can be read in 10 seconds or less. If the text message is any longer it will turn into a distraction, and we don't want any of those!

_____

_____

FRESH TECHNOLOGIES: USE FINANCIAL MANAGEMENT SOFTWARE TO ELIMINATE DEBT SO YOU CAN MAINTAIN FOCUS

Like it or not, your personal finances are among the most important parts of your life. As such, they should rightly occupy a good amount of your attention. If your aspiration involves success as an investor or money manager, perhaps your laser focus is directly trained on personal finance. However, when your focus on personal finance turns into focusing on how to keep up with your monthly bills and avoid drowning in a rapidly rising wave of debt, you have a problem.

So this tip is to help you clear out what might be a current distraction for many of you and may soon be a distraction for many others. This significant distraction can rob you of precious focus time that you can and should be spending on capturing personal and professional success.

To put it bluntly, debt is a killer. While it appears that standards for at least some types of loans and lines of credit are starting to tighten, we live in an era when you can get almost any type of credit you want, regardless of your ability to pay it back. Many creditors secretly hope you can't pay it all back in a reasonable period of time, since they make their greatest profits off the high interest they charge on accumulating debt. To remain adequately focused on the things that matter most in life, you need to eliminate the distraction and stress caused by unnecessary debt and spending.

Fortunately, there are many financial management software programs available that allow you to perform "due diligence" on yourself. Using one of these programs, you can track your daily, weekly, monthly, quarterly, and yearly spending, and figure out where money is being wasted and where savings can be achieved. You would be surprised how much you can save over time by cutting back even on small extras like ordering takeout, buying a morning cup of coffee, or having a drink after work. Software can also help you devise a strategy to gradually pay down your debts so that you eliminate pesky and unnecessary interest charges without bankrupting yourself in the process.

Another advantage of financial planning software is that it can help you see where outsourcing certain tasks you perform can actually save you money. Remember that time is money! Depending on how much you earn per hour, it may actually be cost-effective to pay someone to perform a task such as mowing the lawn, leaving you with time that could produce more value if spent dedicated to your career instead of to household chores.

As long as you are overly distracted by financial matters, you will never be able to fully engage in building your brand and thus will never be able to fully realize your professional and personal potential. So do a little research, select the financial management software that best suits your needs and personal computer system, and get cracking. And remember this motto: Leave no dollar behind!

BROWNIE BITE

To download a focus form, visit www.MyFreshBrand.com.

THE DOGGIE BAG: THE STAYING LASER-FOCUSED TAKEAWAYS

1. It is okay to split your focus into multiple areas, as long as each area directly relates to your aspiration and helps you achieve it. You will probably have to split your focus to some degree, because reaching your aspiration will likely require you to engage in a

variety of activities, acquire a broad range of skills and knowledge, and reach out to a wide network of contacts. Consider each area as a "lens" of your primary focus.

2. When building your personal brand, keep in mind that it needs to be internally as well as externally competitive. Downsizings, restructurings, mergers, and other corporate reshufflings that result in employee reductions are a common occurrence in virtually every industry and you are highly likely to face the possibility of being laid off at least once. You must remain competitive with your co-workers as well as with peers in the outside marketplace. If you do face a layoff situation, remember to remain focused on doing the best job possible and avoid getting distracted by the poor morale and negative employee attitudes that will surround you.

3. Every aspect of Fresh PASSION rests on a foundation of laser focus. Without it, you will never have the discipline or mental toughness necessary to see through the monumental effort that goes into building a top-flight personal brand. Whatever step of Fresh PASSION you are implementing, remember that laser focus needs to be a key part of it.

4. Staying laser-focused means starting with the end in mind. Everything you do should in some way offer a direct step toward your ultimate end goal, and toward making your perfect day a reality. Don't settle for doing something that will lead to a fair approximation of your aspiration, or a second-best version of it. You will have to take many steps to achieve your aspiration, but avoid any step that doesn't somehow tie into your desired end result.

5. Share your focus and commitment with those around you. People are often embarrassed by their goals, fearing that they may not be "good enough" to reach them or that they will be mocked for holding them. You are good enough to achieve whatever you put your mind to, as long as you keep your mind laser-focused. Anyone who would mock your life's aspiration doesn't deserve to be a part of your life. Only by sharing your focus on your

aspiration can you develop the support network that you will need to help make your aspiration into a reality.

6. It is important to create a focus sanctuary where you can take a short rest from your focus and the distractions that pull you away from it. Engage in a pleasurable activity or visit a peaceful place, and allow your mind to relax a bit. This will reduce stress and clear your head of negative thoughts, allowing you to have an even stronger focus when you return.

6.5 Life is full of distractions and temptations that will pull you away from your aspiration. There is no way to realistically eliminate every one of them. You need to have the personal discipline necessary to ignore the distractions that you cannot eliminate. Willpower is critical to maintaining a laser focus. You are only human, but humans are capable of doing great things when they keep their eyes on the prize instead of on short-term gains and pleasures.

6

Fresh PASSION: Selling Your Value

Quotable Notable: Donald Trump

Brownie Point: Never Give Up—The World's Longest Job Interview

Selling Your Value—The Concept, Rationale, and Importance

6.5 Fresh Steps toward Selling Your Value

- **Selling Your Value: Step 1**—Identify and articulate your core strengths and passions so that you understand your value and your ROI.
- **Selling Your Value: Step 2**—Passionately communicate how great you are.
- **Selling Your Value: Step 3**—Communicate with clarity, honesty, and integrity.
- **Selling Your Value: Step 4**—Aggressively pursue personal interactions with people who can help you reach your goals.
- **Selling Your Value: Step 5**—Create your Fresh 10-second text message stating your benefit, value, and ROI.
- **Selling Your Value: Step 6**—Create your Fresh 30-second Super Bowl commercial.
- **Selling Your Value: Step 6.5**—Make it Real and Keep it Fresh—Sell it like you are crazy!

Take Your Pulse: Self-assessment questions measuring your ability to sell your value like you are crazy

It's Showtime!: Daily, weekly, monthly, quarterly, and yearly benchmarks to put your plan into action

Fresh Technologies: Requesting feedback on social networking sites

Brownie Bite

The Doggie Bag: The Selling Your Value Takeaways

> *"People get caught up in wonderful, eye-catching pitches, but they don't do enough to close the deal. It's no good if you don't make the sale. Even if your foot is in the door or you bring someone into a conference room, you don't win the deal unless you actually get them to sign on the dotted line."*
>
> —DONALD TRUMP

QUOTABLE NOTABLE: DONALD TRUMP

Probably the most famous real estate developer in America, Donald Trump has built a fortune that some estimate to be in the billions by developing commercial and residential real estate, casinos, golf courses, and resorts. Trump has also kept his business brand fresh by diversifying into entertainment ventures such as beauty pageants, television shows, and books. With a flair for self-promotion and marketing, Trump has become a pop culture celebrity with a brand based on fierce competitiveness, winning at all costs, and the willingness to create controversy. He went bankrupt in the early 1990s but never lost his focus on or desire for success, and he rebuilt his fortune within a few years. While not universally liked, Trump displays a clear passion to achieve his business and personal aspirations and seems to be living something close to his perfect day.

BROWNIE POINT: NEVER GIVE UP—THE WORLD'S LONGEST JOB INTERVIEW

I was at the National Speakers Association annual convention in July when I received a follow-up phone call from a headhunter I had previously spoken with about an opportunity that he thought I should pursue. Doing my best to block out the noise and distractions around me, I listened as the headhunter explained that the Fortune 5 company, whose position we had previously spoken about, really wanted to interview me on Thursday for what he described as a high-profile management role.

I asked what they were looking for, and he said they wanted a high-profile individual who could come to the company and bring a fresh change management, business growth, and customer service strategy that would enable them to win big time. He went on to say that this company was downsizing, but they realized they had a gap and needed to fill it with a dynamic person who had a track record of results and strong leadership. He further stated that they were being extremely picky about the type of candidates they would even consider for an interview. I immediately went back to my hotel room and started Googling every mention of the company. I went to their website, and I obtained the most recent Moody's and Standard & Poor's reports on them. I basically scoured the Web for anything to understand their strengths and weaknesses, as well as their value proposition, and how I could solve their problems.

Through my research, I saw the company was going through a major shakeup and was in the process of retooling and rechanneling their business. I read an online transcript of a speech the company's CEO had given at Stanford University earlier in the year about their commitment to the environment. I also got hold of the company's previous year-end report and found their strategy for moving forward.

This Fortune 5 retailer was retooling their business model and needed to be able to successfully compete in a dramatically different and more competitive marketplace than they were accustomed to competing in. They also realized that the competition was outperforming them in a number of areas.

Having worked with and competed against many of the types of retailers that would be a threat to them, having led people through major restructuring, having reengineered processes and developed world-class strategies and provided solid servant-style leadership to thousands of directly and indirectly reporting employees, I knew that I could deliver value to this company.

Furthermore, I knew the importance of staying lean and of getting the right people in the right roles with the right tools to deliver on the front line. I had already established a brand as a servant-leader who achieved world-class results with and through people. I was able to do this by articulating a vision and strategy that people could become passionate about and determined to deliver. I also provided the space for them to deliver. In addition, I provided the resources for people to get the necessary skills that would allow them to deliver to the organization while growing personally and professionally. These capabilities, track record, and leadership style became the key point of my selling strategies.

This preparation would come in handy as I embarked on a long and winding journey through what I jokingly like to call the "world's longest job interview." Let me give you a few highlights:

June

I was at the Mercedes dealership getting my car worked on. I called a colleague of mine just to catch him, and he told me that he was thinking about my skills and ability to get results and wanted to connect me with a leadership opportunity in Atlanta. So I interviewed with HR for the position in Atlanta.

July

While attending the National Speakers Association convention in July, I received a call that they wanted to conduct a phone interview for the same leadership position based in Chicago.

Two days later, I conducted the phone interview with an HR rep and the senior leader for the position in Chicago.

Later in July, on vacation with my family in Chicago, I interviewed for a position based in Chicago while they were making a decision about the position in Atlanta. This interview became most stressful because I lost my cell phone signal in the house and had to go outside and take the interview. The only place that I could get a signal was on the edge of the porch next to the gas meter. And every five minutes someone would run out of the house and whisper, "Are you almost done?"

I had dinner with a senior executive to further discuss the positions in Chicago and Atlanta. The conversation seemed to go well. A few days later, an HR representative contacted me who told me they had decided to fill the positions from within but that they wanted to continue the dialogue. I asked what position would we be continuing the dialogue for and he said they weren't sure, but were just sure they wanted to keep talking. I agreed.

August
The HR rep contacted me at the beginning of the month and asked me to come in for an interview for another high-profile executive position on August 11. I would be one of several people interviewing. However, I couldn't make it, so we rescheduled my interview for September.

September
I was scheduled to meet with a vice president and eight leadership team members in mid-September. I spent two weeks individually researching each member of the leadership team to understand their backgrounds, their values, and their pain points. I then prepared a separate interview plan for each person with whom I would be interviewing, aligning different proven aspects of my brand with their exact wants and needs. In each conversation I focused on my brand, my unique ROI proposition, the fresh value and results I could provide, and my track record. After all, past results are the best predictor of future results.

To help myself better understand how my brand related to the needs of their organization so that I would have ready answers about how I could provide value in any possible scenario an interviewer might bring up, I developed a "What If Arsenal," a set of processes and tools to help me through any job interview. By constantly reviewing my skills and experiences and determining exactly how I could leverage them to provide value to a potential employer, I kept my What If Arsenal fresh to keep up with the changing needs of employers, as well as my own changing needs. The What If Arsenal was a weapon that helped me maintain the highest levels of internal and external competitiveness at all times.

Through all this intensive effort, I was able to demonstrate a higher ROI than my competitors, and I was offered the job a week later. All told, I sat through 13 different interviews over a three-month period. During the whole process, I never lost sight of the idea that a job interview is a form of customer service. Your potential employer is the customer and your brand is the product. You need to tailor your brand to the customer's precise needs in order to make the sale. There are many other products on the shelf, so you must have the most competitive brand to sell for the highest value!

To use an example from my earlier life, when I was 15 years old, I began peddling candy and other sweets from a plastic container tucked into my backpack that could be easily displayed to student customers. What began as a small candy business generating about $40 a day blossomed into one that generated $300 to $400 a day and competed with the school's concession stand. I paid attention to what brands and types of candy were most popular and was always willing to keep even a less-popular item in stock if it was favored by one of my steady customers. To say the least, my ability to drive results started very early in life!

And just like I had with my high school candy business, I understood the wants and needs of my customers throughout the "world's longest job interview" and made sure I fulfilled them fairly and honestly.

SELLING YOUR VALUE—THE CONCEPT, RATIONALE, AND IMPORTANCE

Self-promotion is one of the most challenging skills for anyone to master, especially for someone coming right out of school into the workplace.

Self-promotion is an art, not a science. It's the skill of talking about yourself in a way that makes people want to know more. You want them to know in 10 seconds why investing in you (by giving you a job or a contract) is going to benefit them—that's knowing your return on investment (ROI). Remember, your ROI is how much you return on their investment. You have to be able to tell people how valuable you are clearly, consistently, and quickly. No one is going to be interested in your product until they are interested in you.

Remember the three rules of sales: Sell, sell, sell! You're selling yourself, so your brand should represent the very best you have to offer and maximize your innate skills, interests, and strong points. You must believe in the value you bring and what you can do for your sales prospect. Despite the stereotype of the insincere, phony salesperson that makes a killing by telling lies, the reality is that the best salespeople bring genuine passion and confidence to their sales efforts. Frauds always reveal themselves, whether in sales or in any other aspect of life, and being dishonest will do more to damage your brand than almost anything else you do.

You have to identify and define your core strengths and passions, and you have to be able to communicate them clearly and passionately. You need to be able to tell everyone who matters how great you are. You need to make connections with the people you want to sell yourself to, and be able to tell them in 10 seconds why you provide great ROI. You need to always be ready to sell to someone who might help you. Remember that a closed mouth will starve you to death. You must passionately communicate both how great you are and how your greatness will spread throughout any organization you join if you want to dine on your aspirations. In short, you have to find the people who can help you achieve your goals, meet them, wow them, and leave them wanting more.

6.5 FRESH STEPS TOWARD SELLING YOUR VALUE

- *Selling Your Value: Step 1*
  Identify and articulate your core strengths and passions so that you understand your value and your ROI.
- *Selling Your Value: Step 2*
  Passionately communicate how great you are.
- *Selling Your Value: Step 3*
  Communicate with clarity, honesty, and integrity.
- *Selling Your Value: Step 4*
  Aggressively pursue personal interactions with people who can help you reach your goals.
- *Selling Your Value: Step 5*
  Create your Fresh 10-second text message stating your benefit, value, and ROI.

- *Selling Your Value: Step 6*
  Create your Fresh 30-second Super Bowl commercial.
- *Selling Your Value: Step 6.5*
  Make it Real and Keep it Fresh—Sell it like you are crazy!

Selling Your Value: Step 1—Identify and articulate your core strengths and passions so that you understand your value and your ROI

If you are going to sell people on your brand, you need to know what it is. If someone asks you why he should hire *you*, you need to be able to answer in one sentence. This sentence is your definition statement. It must convey what makes you different, distinctive, and competitive, and that you are someone with great ROI. You will use your definition statement during networking, interviews, your 10-second text message, and your 30-second "Super Bowl commercial" (more about these last two items shortly) to alert your current company, the outside world, your customers, and potential and current employers about just how much value your brand truly provides.

Your statement is the foundation that you will build all your communication around. It has to be true to the core of what you do and why you do it well. Without a strong foundation, all your self-promotion and communication will be shaky. You should use your aspirations for your perfect day to hone this statement to a fine edge.

Your statement has to be competitive everywhere. It has to be competitive internally to the company you currently work for (so that you can be awarded with opportunities for leadership positions and promotions, great references, powerful referrals by managers, etc.), as well as competitive externally to the marketplace so that you can attract employers who can award you with a career that is fulfilling both personally and financially. This is critical to gaining exponential personal success internally while developing the professional skills that will keep you competitive on the open market. Having this competitive edge will position you to be able to compete in an economy that is ever-changing and which increasingly demands that current and future employees become more advanced, skilled, and competitive.

Selling Your Value: Step 2—Passionately communicate how great you are

The most effective communication is passionate communication. Once you have created your definition statement, it should reflect your passions. Armed with this passion, it's time to sell like you are crazy. That means not holding back, but rather channeling that passion into your pitch.

This means you have supreme confidence in your fullest potential, and you are constantly searching for new opportunities that will help you meet and even exceed that potential. These opportunities could come in the form of a new job, a promotion, or an award or other form of peer recognition. Whatever the opportunity may be, forget the advice about opportunity knocking. You have to go out knocking on doors—as many as you can find and at all times.

Fortunately, people have a tendency to be passionate about things they have a knack for, so you should always be able to infect others with your passion about what you can do for them. Passion is compelling and passion will give you energy.

You must have passion for your brand. After all, your brand is you, and if you can't work up some passion about yourself, there is a problem there. If you can't be passionate about your brand, why would anyone else be? Never be afraid to be passionate about your brand and how valuable you are. We are taught to be modest and self-effacing. It is considered impolite to brag. But it's not bragging if you can back it up. If you've honed your definition statement to be true to your passions and your strengths, you won't be bragging when you say this is the value you bring to an organization.

If you are excited about your brand, you will be a compelling advocate for your brand. You have to believe passionately in what you sell. Passion can't be faked, and that is part of what makes it so effective. Passion is, by its very nature, honest to itself.

Selling Your Value: Step 3—Communicate with clarity, honesty, and integrity

Remember that your primary goal in developing any type of self-promotion is to deliver fresh, passionate, and engaging communication.

This requires fresh, effective, and engaging communication skills—after all, nobody likes boring! Your communication needs to be clear and concise, and of utmost importance, you must always communicate with honesty and integrity. One of the greatest ways to deliver lasting damage to a brand is to build it on a foundation of dishonesty.

Everyone knows an overaggressive salesperson who is nothing but a slick huckster. These kinds of people give self-promotion a bad name. But if you think about it, you also know what happens to these people's personal brands—they become mud. Once you start down the road of being dishonest in your self-promotion, you have damaged your brand in incalculable ways. People will remember the person they think pulled a fast one on them far longer than they will remember the good things you might have done.

In some ways, this is the single most important thing to remember when crafting your sales strategy. You can always go back and correct errors in how you present yourself, how you demonstrate your value, etc., without serious damage to your brand reputation. But if you make the mistake of being dishonest in how you sell your brand, the resulting damage may prove too great to undo.

Clear, honest communication is effective communication, and you must be an effective communicator. If you can't communicate your brand to people, they won't remember it. If you have any doubts about the importance of how you communicate your brand's unique competitive strengths, bear in mind that academic research supports the notion that those who can communicate well quite simply have a better chance of succeeding in their careers than those who cannot or do not communicate well.

According to "The Importance of Effective Communication," a research paper by Northeastern University professor Edward Wertheim, "People in organizations typically spend over 75 percent of their time in an interpersonal situation; thus it is no surprise to find that at the root of a large number of organizational problems is poor communications. Effective communication is an essential component of organizational success whether it is at the interpersonal, intergroup, intragroup, organizational, or external levels."[1]

---

1. Edward G. Wertheim, "The Importance of Effective Communication," Northeastern University, 1999, http://web.cba.neu.edu/~ewertheim/interper/commun.htm.

Wertheim goes on to say that both expressing and understanding thoughts in the form of words is an extremely complex process fraught with opportunities for error and misunderstanding, made even more complicated by how large a role nonverbal factors (such as body language and tone) play.

By effectively communicating your message both verbally and nonverbally (this is where the confidence and sincerity you exude in every aspect of how you carry yourself comes in), you are arming yourself to solve the root cause of a large percentage of the potential situations that could damage your brand or limit your opportunities for success. Furthermore, considering how widespread communication problems are, imagine the competitive advantage you gain when you become one of the relatively few people who can truly communicate!

Selling Your Value: Step 4—Aggressively pursue personal interactions with people who can help you reach your goals

Now it's time to let the world know who you are.

Once you've defined your ROI and figured out your definition statement, you need someone to tell it to. You can't sell yourself to the walls of your house; you need to go out there and sell your brand to people. Aggressively pursue as many chances for face-to-face interactions with people who can help you reach your goals as possible. You are always increasing your chances for success by coming in contact with more people who believe in your brand. Maybe you've heard of the idea that everyone in the world is only separated by six degrees? That is the power of your network. The more people you connect to directly equals more people you are connected to by only one or two steps.

Someone who can't hire you now but believes in your brand might tell people in his or her network about you. If you've sold your value well enough, other people will sell your value for you. But for your brand to travel down the network, your message needs to be clear, effective, and passionate. The more clarity and power you have when selling your value, the better it will travel from person to person.

There are two sides to aggressively pursuing personal interactions. The first is going out looking for the people who can help you, and the second is always being ready to sell your value to someone helpful whom you didn't expect to meet.

The first case is proactive, and far more important. It's also easier to prepare what you are going to say if you are the one initiating the contact—but you have to find people to pitch to.

Exactly who you need to talk to is going to depend on your brand and your field. You need to research who can help you and where you need to go. But there is some general advice you can follow. Go to career fairs in your field, armed with your brand and knowing how to convey it effectively. If your field has a professional society, joining that is a way to meet people who can help you get ahead. Obviously, a job interview is the essential situation in which you must be ready to sell your value.

It doesn't matter where you find them, but you should always be trying to make contacts. You can sell yourself and your passion best in person. People won't hire you if they don't know you, and you get them to know you by meeting with them. The more you interact with the people who can help you, the more you will expose them to your brand. The more you can reinforce your brand in their minds, the more they will think of you when they have a problem you can solve.

But just because you didn't plan on pitching your brand that day doesn't mean you shouldn't be ready at all times. You should always be ready to tell anyone worth telling about your brand and the value of your ROI. You simply can't predict when you will run into someone who needs to know about your brand. The more you are actively looking for opportunities, the more opportunities you will find. When people see you passionately pursuing this goal, they will start bringing people to you. The more effective your communication is, the more other people will help you. If all your friends and colleagues know your brand, then every time they meet someone who you could bring value to, they are likely to tell that person. They might even arrange a meeting. And while you should never count on it, there is always luck. You might just run into the perfect person while stuck in an elevator or going to a show. There is an old expression, "The harder you work, the luckier you get." If you are prepared to pitch at a moment's notice, then anyone you meet is a chance to promote your brand.

Selling Your Value: Step 5—Create your Fresh 10-second text message stating your benefit, value, and ROI

Your Fresh 10-second text message should be quick, impactful, powerful, compelling, should come at a natural pace, and should convey passion and authenticity. It should quickly answer the question, "Why me?" You'll know that it's successful when the typical response is, "Tell me more." The only way to obtain this response is to sell your brand with confidence and assurance. This text message should be the beginning of every conversation you have about you and your brand. It should be memorable; if it's well done, people will began to refer to you as "the guy that does _____" or "the girl that can _____."

You need to be crystal clear about the benefit that you bring, and you need to be convincingly clear in communicating this benefit. People will immediately ask themselves, "What will he do to make my company better? What would he do to make my life better if I conducted business with him? What kind of experience will he deliver?" Or, they will be looking to quickly answer the question, "Will he provide value or no value?" People will be quick to filter through your verbiage to find the answer. We live in an Internet-speed world where every nanosecond counts; people want to make fast decisions.

You have about 10 seconds to convince a potential employer, client, or network contact of your value. Realizing this, your Fresh 10-second text message should provide no doubt in their minds that you are able to help them meet their individual goals. Don't spin your wheels in the Fresh 10-second text message or explain the details; just state how what you have will bring great results and success, why you are the best person to deliver this benefit, and why you are the standout who can do it better than anyone else. This is a chance for you to state your benefit, value, and ROI, respectively.

When the recipient of your Fresh 10-second text message sees the benefit, value, and great ROI you deliver, they will likely loosen the purse strings and reward you with time, opportunities, and/or resources that will aid your personal and professional success. This Fresh 10-second text message should be evident in your conversations and in your personal advertising and branding material (resume, business cards, correspondence, etc.), as well as during your networking, interviews, etc. Everything that you present should clearly spell out how you can add value and enhance the person's life and/or the organization's performance.

As you gain more experience, you should then revisit your Fresh 10-second text message to ensure that the original buyer (employer) continues to see value in you and gives you the raises, promotions, extra projects, and other perks that can really help you maximize your success and realize your aspirations.

You never know who's scouting for fresh new talent, so be prepared to deliver the Fresh 10-second text message with all potential buyers (you might not be in the market today, but who knows what will happen tomorrow) and let as many potential buyers as possible hear about your brand.

Grab their attention and evoke a response like, "Wow, really? Tell me more..."

Here's how to make this happen (6.5 Fresh Steps). Begin by taking a blank sheet of paper, and then proceed through the following steps:

1. Write down what you have done or want to do that is beneficial to others, whether through work experience, clubs, organizations, civic work, volunteer work, or any other activity. Just write down as many things as possible. Don't worry about the spelling or if it makes sense, just write them down.

    You will be amazed at what you come up with when you put pen to paper. I went back to my college days and devised a text message based on my collegiate career just to show you how no matter where you are in life, you have value that people will pay for and subscribe to. I also want to show you the importance of building the foundation of your brand as early in life as possible. My core values, work ethic, and beliefs have been pretty consistent throughout my life, and as this example will illustrate, many of the core skills and abilities that I developed and solidified in college still serve as a strong base for my brand today. This value will greatly aid your personal and professional success. I started by writing down my achievements.

Michael's College Example

In high school, managed the marketing of my senior class play, the first play in over 20 years for the school. Achieved record attendance for the event and record profits.

Led Phi Beta Lambda, the premier business organization at my university. Achieved record membership within 60 days of assuming the presidency. Raised more money for the organization than the entire student government association's budget. Provided professional development opportunities for seven officers and more than 90 student members.

Helped reduce food costs at my part-time job at Wendy's. The results were a 26 percent reduction in costs and a 34 percent increase in sales for the period, and the general manager rewarded me for my outstanding results.

Awarded President's List status for high scholastic marks (though this is a personal benefit, the sharing of your knowledge will benefit others).

Worked as a summer intern for a youth program. After four weeks of training, I was assigned as co-director for the summer program. Led a team of six instructors and four volunteers. My school received media attention for the design of the program and for helping more than 200 children participate in what was deemed the best summer program around in the area.

Received Student of the Year award during my senior year.

Received top management major award my junior and senior years (based on having the highest GPA).

Worked as a waiter during my junior and senior years for an upscale seafood restaurant. Recognized by manager for outstanding customer service (based on customer feedback) and highest sales for the year.

Delivered results, driven to lead through and with people.

2. Now look over your list and draw a heart around the adjectives (the words that describe something). These heart-drawn words will likely align with the benefits that you can provide. The words will be a large part of the foundation for the sentence that you will write in just a bit.

3. Next, write down the things that you are passionate about. The more things you do that you are passionate about, the greater the results you will be able to deliver and the greater the level of personal and professional success that you will experience because you will pour your heart into it and it won't be boring work for you.

Michael's College Example

(this list is also very similar years later in my professional career):

- HELPING PEOPLE
- EXCEEDING EXPECTATIONS
- WINNING
- TRAVELING
- SERVING OTHERS
- DINING ON ETHNIC FOODS
- ATTENDING LIVE MUSIC AND THEATRE EVENTS
- PRODUCING RESULTS
- PERSONAL GROWTH

4. Now form a fresh, short, and powerful statement from the words that have a heart around them. The minimum word length should be 10 and the maximum should be 13, not counting connective words like "the." Your sentence should be so fresh and powerful that people will want to pay you for the benefit and will remember it long after you have delivered the sentence.

   If you find that the sentence isn't complete, either go back to Step 1 and think some more, or fill in the blank with the benefit that you would like to provide. (However, before you can make this benefit a reality, you will need to go and get the experience and knowledge necessary to enable you to provide the stated benefit.) Think about some famous value statements from fast-food chains, and you will see the clear benefit and that they are memorable: "Making Millions of People Smile" (McDonald's), "Where's the beef?" (Wendy's), or outside the fast-food arena, "We bring good things to life" (GE).

Michael's 10-second text message

"PROVEN LEADER WITH HIGH SCHOLASTIC MARKS WHO HAS A TRACK RECORD OF DRIVING HIGH INDIVIDUAL AND TEAM RESULTS THROUGH AND WITH PEOPLE."

Now use the space here to develop your 10-second text message.

My 10-second text message(s)

_____

_____

_____

_____

_____

What reward do I expect to get for delivering upon the promises in this text message?

_____

_____

_____

5. Use your digital recorder, your voicemail, or whatever recording device you have and record this fresh statement.

6. Send the text message to your friends; put it on your Facebook, YouTube, or Twitter page; call a Branding Board member, or use whatever other communication method you prefer, and get the feedback from your friends, family, colleagues, and Branding Board members. Ask them:

- What benefit did you see in my message?
- Did I sound sincere?
- Was the message fresh?
- If you were in a hiring position, would you hire me?
- What could I do to add more benefit to the message?

6.5 Take the constructive feedback and enhance your message if needed (but stay true to your passion). If your message centers on providing a specific benefit, then hone in on the skills or secure the experience that will enable you to deliver the stated benefit (make sure it is a benefit that you can get paid for).

Selling Your Value: Step 6—Create your Fresh 30-second Super Bowl commercial

When the opportunity presents itself to have a longer conversation and to respond to the "Wow, tell me more," you will need to play your 30-second Super Bowl commercial. This is a spin-off of the Fresh 10-second text message that states the 10-second text message and provides a targeted response to "Wow, tell me more."

Think about this: if you had to do a 30-second commercial about yourself, what would you say? If you met someone on the elevator and had to tell him or her about yourself, what would you say? Would you say something that would get you hired, get you new business, gain a promotion (internally or externally), and/or get someone to follow your leadership?

Companies save their most creative and powerful messaging for commercials that run during the Super Bowl since the Super Bowl is typically the most watched television event of the year. According to Nielsen Media Research, the 2008 Super Bowl was the most watched ever, with 97.5 million viewers. Its ads are the most expensive to buy: a 30-second ad for the 2008 Super Bowl was estimated to cost $2.7 million[2] and companies usually invest the most cost and effort to produce them. Millions are spent on crafting a message that will show distinct value and convince the viewer that they really need a particular product or service.

For many companies, most or all of the year's television advertising dollars are spent during the Super Bowl, since there is no other way to make such a pronounced impact on so many potential customers at once. Super Bowl commercials are also renowned for their creativity, cleverness, and in some cases, edginess. A number of Super Bowl commercials have become classics that are still remembered years later by both the public and the advertising community. That is how powerful the message of a good Super Bowl commercial can be, and that is how important it is to make sure your Super Bowl commercial is engaging, creative, and memorable enough to make a positive brand impression that will last for years in the minds of your audience.

Still not convinced that all this focus on Super Bowl advertising is worth it? Consider that as reported in the Jan. 31, 2005 issue of the television industry publication *Broadcasting & Cable*, Chicago-based media agency Starcom determined that an advertiser could reach more adults ages 18–49 (the primary target audience of most TV ads) at the same cost of running a single Super Bowl ad by running a schedule of ads on competing networks.[3] However, that schedule would require the advertiser to purchase ad time on 381 separate television shows, instead of reaching a huge chunk of audience in one fell swoop. Which method of advertising do you think is more effective in the long run?

Remember your commercial has to be relevant and fresh! I have created several Fresh 30-second Super Bowl commercials that all connect

---

2. "Nielsen's Recap of 2008 Super Bowl Advertising," Nielsen Media Research, Feb. 7, 2008, http://www.nielsenmedia.com/nc/portal/site/Public/menuitem.55dc65b4a7d5adf f3f65936147a062a0/?vgnextoid=697760772bfe7110VgnVCM100000ac0a260aRCRD.

3. Joe Mandese, "Why a commercial during the Super Bowl is worth an unprecedented $80,000 a second," *Broadcasting & Cable*, Jan. 31, 2005, http://www.broadcastingcable. com/article/CA500097.html?display=Feature&referral=SUPP.

to my Fresh 10-second text message, but are customized for the particular audience/individuals (buyers) that I am targeting:

"Hello, my name is Michael D. Brown. I help companies and organizations create and deliver a world-class customer service experience that delivers double-digit growth to the bottom line. I do this while offering a fresh experience and fresh results! The key is to have a leader who can get things done through and with people. I am the person who has a 15-year track record of getting exponential results through and with people." **(I use this while working inside of Fortune 100 corporations and while sharing my value to potential future employers.)**

"Hello, my name is Michael D. Brown. I help individuals get a competitive personal brand so that they are not so generic. It's only when you become a personal brand that you can grow personally and professionally. Through my signature program, Get a Brand or Die a Generic, I prevent individuals from graduating into poverty!" **(I use this in my speaking, coaching, and consulting business.)**

"The number one reason that businesses fail is their stale and poor customer service. And they keep doing the same thing wrong: putting the customer first when really they should be putting the customer second and the employee first. My signature program, Fresh Customer Service, shows them how to put the customer second and the employee first. Doing this leads to customers for life, increased retention, and double-digit growth to the bottom line." **(I use this in my speaking, coaching, and consulting business.)**

Now use the space here to develop your 30-second Super Bowl commercial.

Your 30-second Super Bowl commercial

_____

_____

_____

What reward do I expect to get for delivering upon the promises in this commercial?

Selling Your Value: Step 6.5—Make it Real and Keep it Fresh—Sell it like you are crazy!

You should continue to sharpen your competitive edge even when you're well into your professional career, as you will likely be working in an environment where downsizings, rightsizings, resizings, and economic slowdowns will put your job in jeopardy. My secret weapon (well, it's not a secret anymore because you are reading the book!) to prospering in the modern environment of minimal job security for even high-level executives and proven performers is the commitment to stay fresh and competitive.

Your communication has to stay fresh at all times. Over the course of your career you are going to learn new skills, new approaches, and may even change the focus of your career path while trying to get to your perfect day. Fresh PASSION is about always maximizing what you need to do to succeed. Remember that what you are selling is you. You are your brand, and you are going to change over time. When you change, your communication will have to change. Your 10-second text message right now is not going to be the same as your 10-second text message five years from now.

You have to apply MISS to achieving and maintaining selling your value. Focusing on mindset, image, skills, and substance is that extra half step you need to keep your self-promotion Fresh and yourself competitive.

TAKE YOUR PULSE: SELF-ASSESSMENT QUESTIONS MEASURING YOUR ABILITY TO SELL YOUR VALUE LIKE YOU ARE CRAZY

To keep things fresh and entertaining (and isn't that what selling is all about?), we will measure your answers in this chapter according to a sanity scale. Do you truly sell like you are crazy, or are your efforts all too sane? Answer the following 6.5 questions truthfully according to the following five-point scale (and yes, a five is better than a one!).

Scale

5	♥♥♥♥♥	Strongly agree	That's really, really true about me.
4	♥♥♥♥	Agree	That would be me.
3	♥♥♥	Somewhat agree	50/50 sometimes, sometimes not.
2	♥♥	Disagree	That absolutely has nothing to do with me.
1	♥	Strongly disagree	Let me take the fifth on this.

What's Your Pulse Rate? 6.5 Questions Measuring How You Sell Your Value

1. I have a clear understanding about my worth; I know what I should be paid.

2. I am comfortable with selling the value that I bring.

3. I know and can articulate my ROI.

4. I have made the people who can add to my success aware of the value that I can bring to them and/or their organization.

5. I have a set of skills that is competitive internally (in my job so that I am positioned to receive leadership opportunities, recommendations, and referrals) and externally (in the open marketplace so that I land the career opportunities that are the most rewarding).

6. I have a Fresh 10-second text message and Fresh 30-second Super Bowl commercial that will get me noticed, heard, rewarded, and paid.

6.5 My passion is authentically represented in both my text message and my Super Bowl commercial.

Now that you've assessed yourself, let's analyze your score:

Scores

- **7–13:** You sell your value like you are a sane, vocational person. Rather than examining yourself to find the unique benefit, value, and ROI you deliver, you simply present your basic professional experience and qualifications with a smile and a firm handshake, like you've always been told to. Yawn. Who knew mental health could be so boring?

- **14–20:** You sell your value like you are slightly off-balance. You have probably discovered one or two unique selling points for your personal brand, but you lack any originality in how you get them across to potential customers (i.e., employers and clients).

- **21–26:** You sell your value like you are out there. You are aware of your brand's unique strengths and focus on them in your pitches, but still haven't figured out how to truly differentiate yourself in an ultra-competitive marketplace.

- **27–33:** You sell your value like you are certifiable. You clearly demonstrate your benefit, value, and ROI, and you deliver them in a way that is fresh and engaging for the listener. You have prepared an arsenal to cover the many different scenarios you may be asked to justify your brand against. But you still hang back a little bit. Are you waiting for opportunity to knock instead of kicking down its door?
- **34–35:** You sell your value like you are crazy. Anyone you come into contact with knows about your brand and what it can do in any given situation, and you are constantly refining how you deliver your pitch to make sure your message is fresh and up to date with what you have to offer, what you are looking for, and what best suits the needs of the marketplace. You might be crazy, but you're crazy like a fox!

IT'S SHOWTIME!: DAILY, WEEKLY, MONTHLY, QUARTERLY, AND YEARLY BENCHMARKS TO PUT YOUR PLAN INTO ACTION

You can't just wake up one morning and decide to sell like you are crazy. Think about people who are actually crazy—do they pick and choose when to be crazy, or is craziness embedded into their lives? We don't generally endorse modeling yourself on crazy people, but you get the point. Selling like you are crazy is an activity you must actively partake in on a daily, weekly, monthly, quarterly, and yearly basis. Use the following chart to help you do this.

FREQUENCY	WHAT CAN I DO?	HOW DOES IT HELP MY BRAND?
DAILY	Hear your 30-second Super Bowl commercial out loud—either affirm it to yourself or actually use it in the field.	You need to constantly hear your commercial to make sure you can deliver it with natural ease and that the contents remain fresh and aligned with your aspiration and your capabilities. If you don't have an opportunity to sell your brand to anyone, try selling it to yourself—it's good practice!
WEEKLY	Identify well-known speakers with brands or skills that can help you reach your aspiration and spend an hour either listening to one of their tapes and/or watching one of their videos.	You should constantly energize yourself and obtain fresh ideas and outlooks by seeking out the experiences of people who have already achieved success in your branded field of expertise. While many motivational tapes and videos are less than stellar, there are many good ones, too. Do careful product research to make sure you are only spending time getting quality information from proven successes.
MONTHLY	Give a sample pitch of your 30-second Super Bowl commercial to one Branding Board member and one person you would like to influence (a boss, potential employer, new network member, etc.). Solicit constructive feedback and use it to refine your message.	Beyond your daily affirmation/field testing of your commercial, you also need to rehearse it with an audience qualified to provide you with constructive criticism. This will help ensure your commercial is "real world" ready.

FREQUENCY	WHAT CAN I DO?	HOW DOES IT HELP MY BRAND?
QUARTERLY	Perform an internal "sales review."	You should regard selling your brand in the same way you would regard selling any other high-quality product. Conduct a sales review with yourself, mentally reviewing how many times you pitched your brand, how often you were successful, and what kind of results you achieved. Set quarterly goals and give yourself a bonus if you exceed them. You can also include Branding Board members to get a more thorough review session.
YEARLY	Set goals at an internal "sales meeting."	Every year, you should conduct a full-fledged internal sales meeting where you review your performance from the entire previous year, assess strengths and weaknesses, and set goals for the upcoming year. Include perks and bonuses for exceptional performance. You can also include input from Branding Board members here if you wish.

FRESH TECHNOLOGIES: REQUESTING FEEDBACK ON SOCIAL NETWORKING SITES

With the ubiquity of social networking sites such as Facebook, YouTube, and Twitter, as well as countless blogs and chat rooms devoted to virtually any topic you can think of (and some you probably rather wouldn't think of!), you have the opportunity to painlessly put your Fresh 10-second text message and Fresh 30-second Super Bowl commercial out for public consumption. By downloading an MP3 file of you performing your text message and/or commercial on one of these sites and requesting public feedback, you can get the unfiltered opinions of strangers on just how well your pitch really works.

Naturally, you will get a lot of crank responses, but you will also probably get some honest critiques that you know contain no personal bias. You can even remain anonymous if you choose for better privacy protection.

In addition, there are also a number of sites where you can now post a video resume for review by prospective employers. The video resume is an increasingly popular tool where a job applicant films a pitch explaining their qualifications, rather than submitting a traditional paper resume. Video resumes already stand out from traditional resumes, and your text message and/or commercial can make you stand out even among the trailblazing pack of video resume auteurs.

BROWNIE BITE

Send me an email at speak@themichaeldbrown.com with your 10-second text message or 30-second Super Bowl commercial and I will provide an express critique for you.

THE DOGGIE BAG: THE SELLING YOUR VALUE TAKEAWAYS

1. Selling your value means understanding your return on investment (ROI) and being able to communicate it quickly, consistently, and effectively. Self-promotion is an art, and you must be

ready to sell your brand at any opportunity. When new opportunities arise, you should be able to explain exactly how your brand will allow a prospective employer to reap profits far greater than whatever salary, benefits, and perks they invest in you.

2. You need an effective message for the marketplace in order to support your sales efforts. You must convey what makes you different, distinctive, and competitive (i.e., your brand). This statement is your definition statement. Your statement has to be competitive internally among your colleagues, as well as competitive externally to the marketplace. This is critical to gaining exponential personal and professional success internally while keeping you competitive on the open market.

3. Considering the speed with which business decisions are made today, you need a Fresh 10-second text message that quickly sums up your benefit, value, and ROI. You can use this text message to sell your brand in informal settings, such as an elevator, hallway, or cocktail party, where time is limited and you need to make a powerful impression right away. This text message should be the beginning of every conversation you have about you and your brand, and ideally should leave the other person saying, "Wow, tell me more." Explain how you and your unique abilities will bring great results and success and why you are the best person to deliver this benefit.

4. In addition to a Fresh 10-second text message, you also need to develop a 30-second Fresh Super Bowl commercial. This is built from the Fresh 10-second text message and provides a targeted response to "Wow, tell me more." When devising your commercial, think about this: If you had to do a 30-second commercial about you, what would you say? You can create several different commercials, each one targeting a different aspect of your brand (leadership, creativity, financial results, etc.). You can also individually tailor a commercial to a specific audience. Remember that the commercial has to be relevant and fresh!

5. Communication is a true competitive advantage. Organizations suffer due to poor communications, and without being able to effectively communicate, you will have a difficult time achieving true success, regardless of your branded field of expertise. By properly communicating your brand's unique competitive advantage, you will stand out from the crowd and your message will reach its intended targets in the way it was meant to be received, while most of your competitors will struggle with misunderstandings and lost opportunities to make a sale.

6. You must always communicate with honesty and integrity. One of the greatest ways to deliver lasting damage to your brand is to communicate it using dishonesty. The best salespeople bring genuine passion and confidence to their sales efforts. Frauds always reveal themselves, whether in sales or in any other aspect of life. In some ways, this is the single most important thing to remember when crafting your sales strategy. You can always go back and correct errors in how you present yourself, how you demonstrate your value, etc., without serious damage to your brand reputation. But if you make the mistake of being dishonest in how you sell your brand, the resulting damage may prove too great to undo.

6.5 You must be sure that you present your brand in a way that reflects your true core strengths and passions. When you sell yourself like crazy, you should represent the very best you have to offer and maximize your innate skills, interests, and strong points. Just as you will keep evolving, your self-promotion will have to constantly evolve. Self-promotion is an art, the art of explaining what makes you special, and that will change over time. Always be ready to look at what your brand is now and rework how you sell yourself.

7

Fresh Passion: Invigorating Yourself

Quotable Notable: "Magic" Johnson

Brownie Point: Layoff Lemons to Leadership Lemonade

Invigorating Yourself—The Concept, Rationale, and Importance

6.5 Fresh Steps toward Invigorating Yourself

- **Invigorating Yourself: Step 1**—Understand and embrace the professional standards for your industry, company, business, and/or organization (i.e., appropriate conduct, ethics, and behavior).
- **Invigorating Yourself: Step 2**—Evaluate your three-second impression.
- **Invigorating Yourself: Step 3**—Repeat this exercise with a stranger.
- **Invigorating Yourself: Step 4**—Evaluate your energy level.
- **Invigorating Yourself: Step 5**—Give yourself an emergency booster shot.
- **Invigorating Yourself: Step 6**—Identify a cheerleader who understands the personal and professional success you are aspiring to achieve.
- **Invigorating Yourself: Step 6.5**—Make it Real and Keep it Fresh—Set aside some time for yourself.

Take Your Pulse: Put your finger on the pulse of your vigor and rev up your ambition

It's Showtime!: Understand that invigoration is a constant process, and take daily, weekly, monthly, quarterly, and yearly steps to put your plan into action

Fresh Technologies: Create an innovation blog

Brownie Bite

The Doggie Bag: The Invigorating Yourself Takeaways

> *"I am a businessman. This is what I do each and every day. I love it. I love coming to work. I never have a bad day."*
>
> —Earvin "Magic" Johnson

QUOTABLE NOTABLE: "MAGIC" JOHNSON

NBA Hall of Famer and successful entrepreneur Earvin "Magic" Johnson is a perfect example of how maintaining a high level of vigor can allow you to achieve any aspiration you choose to aim for. Argued by some experts to be the greatest pro basketball player ever, Johnson reinvented the point guard position, was named Most Valuable Player three times, and won five NBA championships during his 14 seasons with the Los Angeles Lakers. After announcing he had contracted HIV in 1991, Johnson refused to slow down. In addition to becoming a national spokesperson for HIV prevention and education, Johnson played on the 1992 gold medal–winning U.S. Olympic basketball team and even made a comeback to play with the Lakers in the 1995–96 season.

Off the court, Johnson became a real estate entrepreneur, specializing in building movie theaters and opening franchise businesses in economically disadvantaged areas that other developers ignored, creating profits as well as improving neighborhoods. And more recently, Johnson became a co-owner of the Los Angeles Dodgers Major League Baseball franchise. By staying invigorated and positive even in the face of serious health issues, Johnson has been able to enjoy continuous personal and professional success throughout his adult life.

BROWNIE POINT: LAYOFF LEMONS TO LEADERSHIP LEMONADE

During many of the downsizings and reorganizations I have survived in my professional career, I always ended up with a promotion or progressive lateral move with increased scope, responsibility, and exposure. I credit this to the valuable and competitive brand that I worked to create and then made efforts to keep fresh, enhance, share, and delivered upon. All this branding work has served me well. Basically, the years of delivering my brand in a way that it could be seen by and experienced by people directly and indirectly has allowed me time and again to take the potentially negative scenario of a corporate reshuffling and obtain positive results.

However, during one of the many downsizings and reorganizations I lived through, I did become a bit nervous. This particular restructuring was said to be one of the largest downsizings in the history of the company. I was most nervous about how my new boss (I will call him Bradley) would represent me in the process of selecting who would be let go and who would remain with the company. Bradley was in his first leadership assignment and was struggling a bit to manage the team. He had only been in his current role and serving as my boss for about three months. He and I hadn't spent much time together.

Further jangling my nerves were rumors that he wasn't fond of my approach, based on an initial encounter that we had where I provided some constructive feedback on his leadership style. He asked for my honest opinion and I told him. I learned a critical lesson from this—although people ask for honest feedback, you need to be careful on the delivery and keep it professional!

According to my colleagues, our new boss thought I had been rude to him. A month later, he and I had a conversation to discuss the rumor. I told him I was sorry if I had come across as rude and that I respected him as my boss and the role that he held. He replied, "I think both of us acted unprofessionally and we should just squash this and move on." We both agreed and walked away. I breathed a little easier but was still far from certain I would still be holding a job after all the layoffs had been announced.

The layoff selection process worked like this:

- The leadership team assembled at the head office with the task of picking the highest-ranking employees and pairing them with the limited roles that would exist in the downsized organization.
- The name of each individual in the organization was put up on a large screen.

- The person's immediate supervisor commented on each individual—speaking of strengths and weaknesses and giving an opinion on whether he or she should remain with the organization. That person's ranking within his or her immediate team was also shared.
- The leadership team would then look at the available positions in the organization and decide the best fit for each employee (if one existed) based on each person's current ranking, skill sets, strengths, and weaknesses.

The process ended after three days. I received a call from my boss and he said, "There are a number of groups in the organization that want you on their team. You need to select from one of the three: Training, Engineering, and Special Projects."

As I stood holding the receiver in my hand, I was baffled and disappointed. I said, "But I have done so well in my role as a district manager and I would like to continue on in this role, as I have worked so hard at obtaining it."

Bradley replied, "Well, these are the choices and you need to let me know now. Oh, by the way, if you don't select one of these roles, you will effectively be tendering your resignation."

I went numb and silent for about two minutes. Finally, I said, "Well, I will take training." He called me back at the end of the day and told me that the training role had been filled and that I had to take the engineering role. I said, "Do you know that I don't know the difference between a screwdriver and a hammer?"

Bradley said, "You take the job or leave it." I immediately said I would take it, but then became so bitter and deflated that I started packing up my laptop and company car keys to turn in to my boss. I was thinking of quitting and feeling distraught.

Shortly after that, my future boss from the engineering team called and congratulated me on my new assignment. Once again, I said, "You know I don't know the difference between a screwdriver and a hammer."

He said, "Michael, we are not looking for someone who can do the actual building. We are looking for someone with strong leadership skills who can help lead the organization through this massive change. We are looking for someone who can get things done and deliver bottom line results. And from what I know and have heard, you are the best candidate."

I said OK and thanked him for the call. I now had two months to transition out of my current role. For the first week, I was bitter with myself, bitter with my colleagues, and bitter with my employees. I began to question my self-worth, question why I had worked so hard to get to this point only to have the rug snatched out from under me.

Two months later, I assumed the engineering role and was still resenting the fact that I was forced to take on a role that I had no background in, and I also feared that I had been set up to fail. I expressed this concern to my new boss and he said I should try to make the most out of the situation.

Here's where I stood: I was remotely located and a thousand miles from my boss. I was told to train with my predecessor (who had been terminated as part of the downsizings); as you can imagine he was not interested in helping me learn the job. After about a month, I decided to pull myself up and do what Michael D. Brown is known for, which is delivering results.

I resolved to prove to myself and the organization that I could be taken out of my comfort zone and still deliver. I reached out to my staff, contractors, and anyone else that I could reach out to for help in learning the new job. About three months later, my boss came out to see me and share praise he had received from the leadership team and our clients about how focused I was and how I was able to solve problems they had been struggling with for years. He said he was giving me high marks in professionalism and customer satisfaction.

This involuntary reassignment was probably the best thing that could have happened to me. My new role had put me on a national stage and given me a level of exposure to the senior leadership team that I couldn't have planned better. In addition, the sudden unexpected risk of losing my job had stoked a fire in my belly and forced me to invigorate myself so that I could maximize the potential of both my personal brand and the new business opportunities that were now available to me. Within seven months of taking on this new role and delivering a consistently high-level, invigorated performance, I was tapped for another role and four more promotions after that.

INVIGORATING YOURSELF—THE CONCEPT, RATIONALE, AND IMPORTANCE

Staying invigorated will give you a huge leg up in making the all-important "three-second impression." In the three seconds it takes you to walk through a door and extend your hand to someone for the first time, that person has already made irreversible judgments about you. You send out hundreds of signals about yourself, and people read those signals and react to them long before you've had a chance to say anything of substance. Success in the new millennium comes to people who are versatile and can make positive impressions in any group. To ensure those judgments are favorable, you need self-confidence, a positive attitude, and a neat appearance.

Remember that the greatest temptation to give up, to slack off, and to lose sight of your goals will come just before you are about to succeed. Stay laser-focused on achieving exponential personal and professional success—whether it is for yourself, your career, your organization, or your business. You must have the tenacity and discipline to go the distance and secure your personal and professional success. Fan the flame within and catch on fire!

6.5 FRESH STEPS TOWARD INVIGORATING YOURSELF

- *Invigorating Yourself: Step 1*
  Understand and embrace the professional standards for your industry, company, business, and/or organization (i.e., appropriate conduct, ethics, and behavior).
- *Invigorating Yourself: Step 2*
  Evaluate your three-second impression.
- *Invigorating Yourself: Step 3*
  Repeat this exercise with a stranger.

- *Invigorating Yourself: Step 4*
  Evaluate your energy level.
- *Invigorating Yourself: Step 5*
  Give yourself an emergency booster shot.
- *Invigorating Yourself: Step 6*
  Identify a cheerleader who understands the personal and professional success you are aspiring to achieve.
- *Invigorating Yourself: Step 6.5*
  Make it Real and Keep it Fresh—Set aside some time for yourself.

Invigorating Yourself: Step 1—Understand and embrace the professional standards for your industry, company, business, and/or organization (i.e., appropriate conduct, ethics, and behavior)

Invigorating yourself begins with taking an energetic, enthusiastic approach to your career. One of the best ways to display this enthusiasm is to thoroughly immerse yourself in the required professional standards.

After you know the standards inside and out, compare them with your current level of professionalism and identify areas of opportunities for you to strengthen your presentation and areas where you need to quickly acquire the standards. You will have a renewed appreciation for your chosen field of expertise and a competitive edge that will fill you with vigor for success and advancement. Without this first step, any invigoration you achieve will be misapplied and ultimately wasted, as the potential for career-killing inappropriate actions and words will surely trip you up sooner or later.

Invigorating Yourself: Step 2—Evaluate your three-second impression

In addition to allowing you to fully embrace the standards of your chosen field of expertise, staying invigorated will also give you a huge leg up in making the all-important "three-second impression." As mentioned earlier, in the three seconds it takes you to walk through a door and extend your hand to someone for the first time, that person has already made irreversible judgments about you. You send out hundreds of signals about yourself, and people read those signals and react to them long before you've had a chance to say anything of substance. Ask your friends, colleagues, and/or Branding Board of Advisers to close their eyes and open them when you walk into the room and give their first impression of you. Compare this impression with your intended impression and work on closing the gaps.

Remember, success in the new millennium comes to people who are versatile and can make positive impressions on any group. To ensure people's judgments about you are favorable, have self-confidence, a positive attitude, and a neat appearance. None of these traits is possible without a constant flow of vigor and confidence that exudes from you and is obvious to everyone you come in contact with. So stay invigorated and make those first three seconds meaningful!

> *"You can't see the big picture if you are in the frame. Get help from someone who can tell you what you need to hear."*
>
> —MICHAEL D. BROWN

Invigorating Yourself: Step 3—Repeat this exercise with a stranger

While I would not advise walking up to the next person you see on the street and asking for a three-second first impression review, you can certainly conduct this exercise with someone you meet at a professional or charitable event, or perhaps someone you have never met before who knows one of your friends, relatives, or colleagues. Offer to reciprocate the exercise and give your critique of their three-second impression in order to increase the shared value. Once again, compare this impression with your intended impression and work on closing the gaps.

Invigorating Yourself: Step 4—Evaluate your energy level

Ask your friends, colleagues, managers, and/or Branding Board of Advisers to select one of the following four categories to describe your energy level:

A. Energetic and ready to move.

B. Sluggish and unsure.

C. Confident and alert.

D. Unsure.

Get multiple opinions, and try to include different people whose points of view you know rarely coincide. If you receive mostly or all "A" and "C" ratings, your energy level is probably in pretty good shape. If you get any "D" ratings, your energy level may be in good shape, but you need to work on how you convey it to the outside world.

Even one or two "B" ratings indicate a potentially serious problem with your energy level. If you are properly invigorated, nobody should be able to mistake your vigor for sluggishness or lack of surety in yourself. Don't become disheartened if you do get some "B" ratings; use the situation as an opportunity to go back and repeat the first three steps, paying extra-close attention for clues as to where exactly your energy level is sagging and what you may be able to do to jolt it back to an acceptably high voltage.

Invigorating Yourself: Step 5—Give yourself an emergency booster shot

Even the strongest, most highly charged battery will start to wear down if it runs at full capacity for long enough. From time to time, your own Fresh PASSION battery may falter a bit. Properly following all the steps in this book is an undertaking that requires enormous amounts of time, energy, and dedication—but the reward is exponential. While many of the brand-building activities I describe are contagious and create their own energy that you can feed off, you will still occasionally find yourself understandably exhausted from the challenge of reaching for your highest personal and professional aspirations.

At these times, you need to give yourself an "emergency booster shot," which is a non-brand, non-career-related activity you can partake in to step away from the grind and quickly reinvigorate yourself. An emergency booster shot can be a walk in the park, a game of golf, a matinee movie, a dinner with a friend, a concert, or even something more involved such as a well-deserved week's vacation at the beach (if you can afford it!). Your emergency booster shot can basically be anything that is positive, enjoyable, and allows you to take a short break from your brand without becoming a distraction or obstacle. You will be surprised how much more energetic and excited you are about your brand after spending a little time away from it!

Invigorating Yourself: Step 6—Identify a cheerleader who understands the personal and professional success you are aspiring to achieve

This cheerleader can be a part of your Branding Board or a totally different individual. Most important is that they have walked in your shoes and gotten somewhere during that journey. It is one thing for a friend who may know you quite well personally, but knows nothing about your chosen field of expertise, to tell you that you're on the right track and have what it takes to succeed. It's another thing to hear that message from somebody who is intimately familiar with your chosen field of expertise and can give you specific insights about what you're doing right—and what you could be doing better. Just make sure this person isn't someone who lacks the ability to motivate a three-year-old even if you paid them!

Invigorating Yourself: Step 6.5—Make it Real and Keep it Fresh—Set aside some time for yourself

Invigorating yourself is all about maintaining a high level of energy and professionalism at all times. Sad to say, this will clearly set you apart from the everyday American worker. How do you obtain and then maintain this high energy and enthusiasm? By having fun, of course!

As opposed to Step 5, which involves stepping away from your career to take an emergency booster shot of something fun, Step 6.5 involves having fun in your studies and career-building activities. Obviously, we are talking about fun within rational limits—treat your job as one big party, and you will not go far. But by approaching the professional part of your life with a lighthearted, enthusiastic attitude, you will find it much easier to pour your heart into your goals and aspirations.

The new, invigorated you will spill over into your professional life, personal life, during networking with peers, during job interviews and performance reviews, and any other time you can think of. Keep in mind that misery already has enough company and that companies definitely don't like misery, so stay invigorated throughout the journey.

TAKE YOUR PULSE: PUT YOUR FINGER ON THE PULSE OF YOUR VIGOR AND REV UP YOUR AMBITION

How invigorated are you? Is your heart proudly pumping enthusiasm and confidence throughout your body, or is it timidly tapping sluggishness and lack of commitment? Answer the following questions using the scale of one to five hearts and find out if your vigor levels need "topping off."

Scale

5 ♥♥♥♥♥	Strongly agree	That's really, really true about me.
4 ♥♥♥♥	Agree	That would be me.
3 ♥♥♥	Somewhat agree	50/50 sometimes, sometimes not.
2 ♥♥	Disagree	That absolutely has nothing to do with me.
1 ♥	Strongly disagree	Let me take the fifth on this.

What's Your Pulse Rate? 6.5 Questions Measuring How You Invigorate Yourself

1. I clearly understand what the professional standards are for my desired industry.
2. My three-second impression is in alignment with how I want to be viewed.
3. My energy level and enthusiasm is high.
4. I am generally an invigorated person.
5. I know what makes me happy.
6. I frequently inject something fun into my day, week, month, and year.

6.5 I know how others view me within the first three seconds.

Now that you've taken the test, let's analyze your score:

Scores

- **7–13:** You are apathetic. You lack enthusiasm for building your brand or reaching your aspirations. Since achieving any type of success requires vigor, you probably frequently experience failure, which saps your energy even further, creating a vicious downward cycle. Break the cycle today! Go back and read this chapter again, and start implementing its advice. You won't completely change overnight, but if you apply genuine passion and determination toward building your brand and realizing your aspirations, you will be surprised by how fast you start to see incremental improvements.
- **14–20:** You are mildly enthused. As opposed to someone who is truly apathetic, you at least have goals for your brand and your aspirations in mind, but you lack the vigor to pursue them in any real way. Your mindset may be a little healthier than that of your apathetic colleagues, but your results will not likely be much better. You should give this chapter a second look and try to make some positive changes based on what you read.

- **21–26:** You are interested. Beyond merely holding goals, you possess some genuine energy and gumption to meet them. But your commitment to achieving true success is still suspect. You are probably willing to take shortcuts and accept results that are "pretty good" or "not perfect but close." You have what it takes to meet a portion of your personal and professional potential, but you're leaving a lot of achievable success on the table.
- **27–33:** You are impassioned. You have a great deal of energy to dedicate to building your brand and realizing your aspirations, and also a lot of genuine passion to follow all the necessary steps and hold out for full results. But the finish line is a long way off, and there are many chances to stumble and fall before you reach it. Training for a marathon is one thing, completing it is another, winning it is something else entirely.
- **34–35:** You are invigorated. Every ounce of physical and mental energy at your disposal is committed to building your brand and achieving your aspirations, and you have enough energy to power a small city. You match that energy with boundless passion that allows you to focus with laser intensity on everything you need to do to maximize your full potential. Everyone around you senses your vigor, and it is contagious. You exert a positive influence on others simply by the way you wholly dedicate yourself to making your perfect day a reality.

IT'S SHOWTIME!: UNDERSTAND THAT INVIGORATION IS A CONSTANT PROCESS, AND TAKE DAILY, WEEKLY, MONTHLY, QUARTERLY, AND YEARLY STEPS TO PUT YOUR PLAN INTO ACTION

Invigorating yourself is a constant process. You cannot simply declare yourself invigorated and then check off some little vigor box and be done with it (or you can, but you'll only be fooling yourself!). Vigor, like any form of energy, needs to be recharged, replenished and renewed. Take a look at the following chart for tips on how to stay invigorated on a daily, weekly, monthly, quarterly, and yearly basis.

FREQUENCY	WHAT CAN I DO?	HOW DOES IT HELP MY BRAND?
DAILY	Take a step "outside the zone" and do something good for yourself or a friend, family member or colleague.	Spending a few minutes a day treating yourself or someone close to you right will boost your self-esteem and confidence, which in turn will fuel your vigor. Surprise a colleague with a healthy treat, or carve time in the day to read a chapter of a favorite novel.
WEEKLY	Have a brief cheerleading session.	Get in touch with your personal and professional success cheerleader to obtain a few "rah rahs." This can be accomplished via text message, email, or other virtual link, as well as by phone or in person. Something as simple as an inspirational email message listing three easy steps you can take to get closer to reaching your aspiration can provide a huge dose of vigor.
MONTHLY	Allow yourself an agendaless day.	Pick a weekend day, holiday, or vacation day where you will wake up with no concrete goals or plans other than enjoying the day. Free flow it, and don't be afraid to "waste" time doing things like people-watching or window-shopping. When you return to your agenda the following day, you will have enough vigor to complete it twice.

FREQUENCY	WHAT CAN I DO?	HOW DOES IT HELP MY BRAND?
QUARTERLY	Get your quarterly "emergency booster shot."	Your emergency booster shot can basically be anything that is positive, enjoyable, and allows you to take a short break from your brand without becoming a distraction or obstacle. You can administer these shots "as needed," but you should take one at least once a quarter, even if you're feeling healthy! You will be surprised how much more energetic and excited you are about your brand after spending a little time apart from it!
YEARLY	Allow yourself an agendaless week.	Everyone deserves a vacation! Take one week out of the year (during a semester break) and forget about your brand. Whether you travel to a foreign country, never leave your backyard, or go somewhere in between, pursue fun activities and loosen up a little. When you return, you should have enough spare vigor to carry you through the next year!

Text Message

Keep your vigor flowing by composing a text message that describes how you invigorate yourself to stay fresh and passionate in your approach to building your brand and realizing your aspirations. Writing out a long, protracted text message will sap your vigor and waste energy that could be better spent elsewhere, so make it quick and snappy!

_____

_____

FRESH TECHNOLOGIES: CREATE AN INNOVATION BLOG

You can create a steady stream of bubbling innovation by creating a blog. Create an innovation blog dedicated to brainstorming new and creative approaches to your schoolwork, extracurricular activities, internships and co-ops, and other career-building activities. In addition to posting your own thoughts, you can invite friends, relatives, colleagues, and network members to participate. Open your blog up to public comment to further expand the depths from which innovation can bubble up!

BROWNIE BITE

Have you subscribed to our award-winning newsletter? This is a free, powerful, monthly tool that is packed with value and substance. Just go to www.MyFreshBrand.com and sign up.

THE DOGGIE BAG: THE INVIGORATING YOURSELF TAKEAWAYS

1. Even a negative work experience can invigorate you to succeed in future endeavors. Tyrannical professors and bosses teach you how to stay on your toes and deliver results in the most difficult of circumstances, lazy project partners and coworkers force you

to shoulder larger workloads than you ever thought you could possibly carry, and overly demanding customers instill in you reserves of patience and diplomacy you never knew you possessed. With the right attitude, you can leave a bad job or academic situation with renewed confidence, as well as a burning desire to improve your fortunes and move on to better things!

2. To gain the benefits of invigorating yourself, you must be immersed in the standards of your profession. Regardless of how much energy, enthusiasm, and passion you possess, unless you know how to properly act and present yourself in a given situation, you will not succeed. Make sure your level of professionalism matches your level of vigor.

3. In the three seconds it takes you to walk through a door and extend your hand to someone for the first time, that person has already made irreversible judgments about you. You send out hundreds of signals about yourself, and people read those signals and react to them long before you've had a chance to say anything of substance.

4. Remember, success in the new millennium comes to people who are versatile and can make positive impressions in any group. To ensure people's judgments of you are favorable, have self-confidence, a positive attitude, and a neat appearance. None of these traits is possible without a constant flow of vigor and confidence that exudes from you and is obvious to everyone you come in contact with. So stay invigorated and make those first three seconds meaningful!

5. Properly maintaining the highest levels of vigor requires periodically stepping away from building your brand and achieving your aspirations and having a little "me" time. This includes simple daily activities such as taking five minutes to have a healthy snack, as well as more involved, less frequent activities such as attending a sporting event or even taking a week's vacation. Even the strongest battery needs to be recharged, and even the sun will burn out if it shines long enough without any break.

6. Create an innovation blog dedicated to brainstorming new and creative approaches to your career-building activities. Invite colleagues and strangers to participate in creating a continuous stream of bubbling innovation.

   The greatest temptations to give up or slack off will often occur right before you achieve your success. Staying invigorated is the difference between going those last few miles and giving up when the race is 90 percent complete. "Pretty good" results are fairly easy to obtain; "great" results are extremely difficult. Yet with a little more vigor, many people with "pretty good" lives could live great ones instead.

6.5 One of the most important aspects of vigor is having fun. Apply a lighthearted attitude to even your most difficult tasks and don't be afraid to find ways to enjoy what may otherwise be tedious tasks. You can't take a "party all the time" attitude and sometimes professionalism requires a serious demeanor, but you will find yourself far more invigorated when you're having fun and interested in what you're doing than when you're miserable and bored.

8

Fresh Passion: Omitting the Negative

Quotable Notable: Tyler Perry

Brownie Point: If You Thought Presidential Politics Were Tough, Check Out The Office

Omitting the Negative—The Concept, Rationale, and Importance

6.5 Fresh Steps toward Omitting the Negative

- **Omitting the Negative: Step 1**—Face the pain that inevitably comes along on the way to success, but don't let it consume you.

- **Omitting the Negative: Step 2**—Allow yourself pleasure, but remember you can have too much of a good thing.

- **Omitting the Negative: Step 3**—Strive to be the best, but don't let pressure cloud the fact that you are a fallible human being who will not always be number one.

- **Omitting the Negative: Step 4**—Learn to recognize persecution so you can avoid it, not succumb to it.

- **Omitting the Negative: Step 5**—Placate yourself to be mentally prepared at all times for negativity—Negativity is unavoidable.

- **Omitting the Negative: Step 6**—Persevere through whatever negativity you experience.

- **Omitting the Negative: Step 6.5**—Make it Real and Keep it Fresh—Maintain your professionalism at all times.

Take Your Pulse: Put your finger on the pulse of your openness to negativity

It's Showtime!: Commit to the constant battle of overcoming negativity, and take daily, weekly, monthly, quarterly, and yearly steps to put your plan into action

Fresh Technologies: Increase the computing power of your brain

Brownie Bite

The Doggie Bag: The Omitting the Negative Takeaways

> *"I was unhappy and miserable during the first 28 years of my life. The things that I went through as a kid were horrendous. And I carried that into my adult life. I didn't have a catharsis for my childhood pain, most of us don't, and until I learned how to forgive those people and let it go, I was unhappy."*
>
> —TYLER PERRY

QUOTABLE NOTABLE: TYLER PERRY

Successful playwright, actor, and director Tyler Perry suffered significant physical and emotional abuse during a childhood marked by poverty in New Orleans. Following years of struggle as an unknown playwright, Perry began achieving recognition for his work in the late 1990s after he omitted his negative childhood experiences from his life and allowed himself to focus solely on building his personal brand. Today Perry is a show business mogul who has branched from plays into films, television, and books. Truly representing the "do it yourself" ethic of Fresh PASSION, Perry built his brand with virtually no outside assistance, relying on word-of-mouth and self-produced online marketing to develop an audience that has steadily grown and remained loyal during the past decade.

> *"Absolutely no one's negative acts or words can have an impact on you without your permission."*
>
> —MICHAEL D. BROWN

BROWNIE POINT: IF YOU THOUGHT PRESIDENTIAL POLITICS WERE TOUGH, CHECK OUT THE OFFICE

I still have the day and time saved in my Outlook calendar. It was March 7 at 1:25 p.m. It was cold outside and drizzling rain. I had just arrived at a client location from having lunch at one of my favorite Japanese restaurants, the taste of Miso soup still fresh in my mouth. My cell phone rang, and I briefly looked down at the phone. Normally I don't answer the phone when I am with a client, but when I saw that it was our senior vice president, I asked my client to excuse me for a minute.

I ventured back outside into the brisk cold weather and listened to the senior vice president as he said, "Michael, I want to thank you for all of your hard work."

I simply replied, "You're welcome," as I thought he was talking about a presentation that I had given the past week in his presence. But as it turned out, he was talking about something a lot bigger than a single presentation.

"Michael," he continued, "I would like you to join my leadership team as a regional operations manager. This is a very big role, and you will have a pretty big organization to run." The actual numbers involved would be about 150 sites, 15 people on my leadership team, and 1,000 employees in my organization.

I went numb for a minute, although I had been aspiring for a senior leadership role when I started with the company several years earlier. I knew that I would eventually get the role, but I had honestly expected it to come in about three more years. So he asked if I would be willing to take this role, and I said yes. He said he would be back in contact with me to discuss the transition.

I hung up the phone and started shaking, thinking to myself, *I can't believe this just happened to me, something I have been aspiring to for a very long time has come when I least expected it and much quicker than I had ever imagined.* I went to bed that night excited and very nervous, worrying about what a huge assignment I had accepted and doubting whether I was really ready for it. This particular leadership role was highly coveted in the company and was usually awarded to people whose tenure was about five to six years longer than mine at that point.

But I knew from previous experience that being anything other than confident was not an option. So a month later, I transferred to the home office to begin my assignment. When I got on the elevator, an employee whom I had briefly met two years earlier said, "Michael, I am not sure what is going on—there are people who are in an uproar about your appointment. They are saying you are too young, that you are too new to this part of the country, and that you don't have enough experience for this big role. They are really mad that the role wasn't given to Chuck (as I will call him), who is much more seasoned than you and has worked really hard and was promised this role." She went on to say that she had told them she had met me and I seemed like a really nice guy who deserved a chance. I didn't have a great feeling about how effective that plug for me had been.

I stepped off the elevator into the office and I could feel the tension in the air settling in my lungs. There were no congratulations, just stares. The stares soon expanded into people asking me blatantly, "How did you get the new role?"; "Why did they choose you over Chuck who knows this business and has been here for a long time?"; and my favorite, "I don't think you know what you are getting into. They are setting you up for failure."

Rather than trying to justify my presence or rebut anyone's challenge, I simply replied, "Thank you for your support and I am sure with the right support team I will be just fine."

Despite my cool exterior demeanor, inside I crumbled for a little while. Here I had shed blood, sweat and tears and worked really hard over the last nine years to get the required skills, produce top quarterly results, and provide a level and style of leadership that was world-class. I thought people would be happy for me, but instead they were bitter and questioned my qualifications. And I think most of all, they assumed that I had done something to prevent someone they uniformly loved and respected from obtaining a role that they thought he was better qualified for and deserved.

For the first couple of months, the backstabbing and negative water cooler conversations about me continued and people were not shy about voicing their opinion. I went to Chuck and said to him that I apologized if he thought that I had done anything to prevent him from getting what had become my role. I went on to tell him that I had never applied for the role, but had been appointed by the senior vice president. Chuck assured me that he didn't have a problem with me and we shook hands and parted.

I left the office that day and swore that I would overcome this negative and hostile environment and just deliver top-notch results with and through people, the very people who wanted nothing more than to see me fail as spectacularly as possible. I met with my team later that week, and even they were skeptical that I could overcome this intensely politicized situation. I spent a solid month visiting with everyone who directly reported to me and with all the other employees in my 1,000-plus-person organization. My intent was to just listen and hear what was in their hearts and on their minds, thank them for what they had done in the past, and thank them for what they would do in the future for my organization and the company as a whole.

I had worked too hard to build my brand and prove my value and had dug down deep to pour too much Fresh PASSION into my career to now let petty office politics prevent me from realizing my aspiration of leading a large organization and obtaining results with and through people. I stayed laser-focused on delivering positive results and omitting all of the negativity that was threatening to derail me.

How did everything turn out? You will see the final results in the next chapter, "Nailing the Brand." Suffice it to say that I did not write this book to provide you with an example of how negativity and close-mindedness can overcome a passionate effort to build a brand and realize your greatest aspirations!

OMITTING THE NEGATIVE—THE CONCEPT, RATIONALE, AND IMPORTANCE

I don't need to tell you that negativity surrounds you in this world, whether you are in college or in the professional arena. Even emanating from your friends, family, and colleagues, it is all around. Your job will be to not waste your precious time and resources dealing with negativity. Remember, you are building a foundation that will lead to a stellar career with opportunities for enhancement, a thriving business, or a new venture. You simply don't have time to waste. Omitting the negative will be an extremely useful skill that you should carry with you throughout your professional and personal life.

When you encounter a negative experience—learn from it. Don't spend a lot of time dwelling on it—you don't need to let it consume valuable real estate in your head, because you have so much more ahead of you.

Of course, you must realize that success is not a day at the beach in Maui, sitting on a reclining chair, watching the pounding surf, and drinking a Long Island Iced Tea full of aspirations. There will inevitably be negatives that come your way, and omitting them will not always be an easy task.

In particular, you will have to successfully deal with the dreaded "P4"—pain, pleasure, pressure, and persecution. On this journey to personal and professional success you will have to deal with these four major obstacles and your challenge will be to not let any of this derail you. P4s will be potentially negative derailments to your personal and professional success journey. They have a strong potential to have a negative impact, and the way in which you tackle and overcome these potential derailments is critical to your obtaining and sustaining success.

You must go through each aspect of P4 to learn from them, but don't let them lead you, consume you, or cause you to lose focus. You will need to omit these potential negatives both proactively and reactively. Find the lessons that all this negativity can teach you and use them to write the next successful chapter. Do it right and pretty soon you will be experiencing exponential personal and professional success.

6.5 FRESH STEPS TOWARD OMITTING THE NEGATIVE

- *Omitting the Negative: Step 1*
  Face the pain that inevitably comes along on the way to success, but don't let it consume you.
- *Omitting the Negative: Step 2*
  Allow yourself pleasure, but remember you can have too much of a good thing.

- *Omitting the Negative: Step 3*
  Strive to be the best, but don't let pressure cloud the fact that you are a fallible human being who will not always be number one.
- *Omitting the Negative: Step 4*
  Learn to recognize persecution so you can avoid it, not succumb to it.
- *Omitting the Negative: Step 5*
  Placate yourself to be mentally prepared at all times for negativity—Negativity is unavoidable.
- *Omitting the Negative: Step 6*
  Persevere through whatever negativity you experience.
- *Omitting the Negative: Step 6.5*
  Make it Real and Keep it Fresh—Maintain your professionalism at all times.

Omitting the Negative: Step 1—Face the pain that inevitably comes along on the way to success, but don't let it consume you

The journey to personal and professional success can sometimes be painful. You will experience some roadblocks, and you will experience some hurt and disappointments inflicted by people you thought cared about you. There will be days and nights where you will feel like you hit a brick wall, and some days where you will be dealt some defeats. There will be days where you just want to cry, or even days when you give in to your emotions and cry real tears.

Does this sound all too familiar? Relax. The pain is normal and should be expected. What you will absolutely not do is let this pain consume you. Instead, you must extract the valuable lesson hidden within the pain, learn what went wrong, and put mitigations in place to prevent the reoccurrence and/or minimize the effect that it can have on your journey to personal and professional success. Remember that it is impossible to avoid mistakes, but not impossible to avoid the same mistakes twice!

***Omitting the Negative: Step 2**—Allow yourself pleasure, but remember you can have too much of a good thing*

Most of us would like to spend our days galloping in the pleasures of life—attending a party where the conversation flows freely and the responsible beverage of your choice even more freely, going on a shopping spree every Saturday, volunteering at your favorite charity, taking a trip to Europe, or basking in the Key West sun for days on end. It is great to seek out the pleasure in life and we should have this on our "to do" list. But that list can get awfully crowded.

What you must not do is partake in pleasure at the expense of not achieving your aspirations, not acquiring the skills necessary to become a branded expert, not enhancing your brand, not broadening your network, not building your Branding Board of Advisers. You must be disciplined and deliberate in planning what pleasures to partake in and when to partake in them on your success journey. Too much of a good thing too much of the time leads to too little personal and professional success. This also slows your progress and the speed with which you are able to realize success.

***Omitting the Negative: Step 3**—Strive to be the best, but don't let pressure cloud the fact that you are a fallible human being who will not always be number one*

The pressure to be the best and to always win is enormous in this country. Some pressure is necessary. Without it you will not have the great inner drive you'll need to make the enormous effort that leads you to true success. But the pressure brought on by your peers, colleagues, family, and friends can be nerve-wracking and can serve as a serious roadblock to your success.

That's why it is critical to understand the true nature of your aspirations and the brand you are attempting to create. Properly executing on your core aspiration and brand will make it easier for you to excuse yourself from the negative pressure dished out to you. Instead, you will be able, with a clear and relaxed mind, to subject yourself to the good and purposed pressure that is applied to you by your Branding Board of Advisers and members of your network, yourself, friends, and colleagues to whom you have clearly articulated both your aspirations and the fresh and competitive branded expert that you are seeking to become.

They should also be made aware that you have no interest in being a generic brand, so the good pressure that they put on you should be targeted to help you become that fresh and competitive branded expert who is seeking to capture personal and professional success as a result.

Omitting the Negative: Step 4—Learn to recognize persecution so you can avoid it, not succumb to it

Let me tell you a secret (don't tell anyone): not everyone wants to see you gain personal and professional success. This can include people you view as your "friends," as well as colleagues, family, partners, etc. And the more successful you become, the stronger the persecution is likely to be.

Now that you realize this little secret of life, it is your job to let any persecution you encounter roll off you like water off a duck's back. Don't waste your precious and valuable time ingesting this persecution. Listen to it once, extract any lessons (i.e., stay away from certain people in the future), and move on.

Give your persecutors this rehearsed statement—"I thank you for thinking enough of me to take time out of your business schedule to provide me with what you think and believe to be valuable feedback. Thank you for thinking of me." Then walk away and never look back!

Omitting the Negative: Step 5—Placate yourself to be mentally prepared at all times for negativity—Negativity is unavoidable

There is a fine line between having a healthy state of preparation for negativity whenever and wherever it may pop up and having an unhealthy sense of paranoia or resignation about the negative side of life. To stay on the right side of this line, you need to placate yourself with the knowledge that while negativity is inevitable, being defeated by negativity is far from inevitable.

Placation is essentially the act of appeasement or conciliation. So appease yourself. When you find yourself nervous or scared about being overcome by negativity, remind yourself that you are prepared enough and strong enough to handle whatever obstacles come your way. Maybe link this positive mental reinforcement to an activity, such as a workout session at the gym or even a five-minute stroll away from your desk. And any time you find yourself feeling confident that you can handle whatever negativity may arise, reinforce that thought by giving yourself a small reward, such as eating a healthy snack or taking time to read an interesting magazine article.

In this way, you will placate yourself and also mentally train yourself to only have "positive" feelings about your ability to handle negativity. I'm not asking you to be a Pollyanna—you will experience negativity, and probably plenty of it! But with the right placation and mental preparation, you will wade right through it and come out unscathed.

Omitting the Negative: Step 6—Persevere through whatever negativity you experience

Step 5 is about preparing yourself for the negativity you will experience. Step 6 is about surviving the negativity you will experience. Perseverance is steadfastness in the face of what may seem to be overwhelming adversity. Perseverance wins wars and holds families and nations together in times of crisis. It also allows careers to flourish in situations where there is covert or overt hostility and resistance.

While some people may innately possess higher levels of perseverance than others, ultimately it is a trait that is made, not born. With mental commitment and dedication, anyone can successfully persevere through virtually any amount of negativity and opposition. How do you build perseverance? Fortunately, by following the steps of Fresh PASSION, you will naturally strengthen your perseverance muscles and develop the toughness and self-discipline your journey toward success will require.

How is this so? Because by gearing your whole life toward your brand and your aspirations, you are accepting that they rank with the most important aspects of your existence and are devoting an enormous amount of time and effort into achieving them. (Family, health, and spirituality are the only things that should take precedence.) When you stake your life on something, you become willing to fight for it with all your might. You will obtain the perseverance necessary to overcome any amount of negativity without even realizing it. But this will only happen if you truly dedicate yourself to Fresh PASSION. Pay lip service, and when the chips are down, you will find yourself holding a weak hand. Truly devote yourself and you will be dealt a royal flush every time you place a bet.

Omitting the Negative: Step 6.5—Make it Real and Keep it Fresh—Maintain your professionalism at all times

You will need to fight against negativity, and fight hard, to fully build your brand and achieve your aspirations. But remember that you must fight fair and fight subtly. When you find a knife in your back, the natural inclination is to stick it right between the shoulder blades of the person who stuck it there. Resist the temptation.

Instead, learn as much as you can from this backstabbing experience. How and why did you allow someone to betray you? What was their motivation, and what clues did you miss? Rather than lowering yourself to their level and devising a sneaky, underhanded response, rise above them and defeat them by working harder, producing better results, and delivering better value. And the next time they or someone else tries to stick the knife in, you will effortlessly slide out of harm's way and leave them stabbing at empty air.

Betrayal and sabotage can produce short-term gains, but people who try to get ahead deviously quickly hit a ceiling and never realize their full potential. Long-term, permanent success only comes to those who dedicate themselves to their brand and their aspirations and prove their own worth without trying to sully anyone else's.

At the end of the day, all you have is your reputation. Your brand totally relies on it. Do you want your brand to be based on the reputation of someone who is combative, who holds a grudge, who is quick to lash out at perceived slights, and who seems to have many enemies? Or would you rather build your brand based on the reputation of someone who always carries a cool, calm demeanor, who stays above the fray, and who speaks more loudly with actions that deliver value than anyone can with negative words?

Professionals don't engage in petty feuds or adolescent revenge schemes, and as mentioned earlier, it's never too early to start acting and thinking professionally. Certainly stand up for yourself, but do so in an adult, rational manner. Medieval poet George Herbert is credited with the saying, "Living well is the best revenge." Let that be your mantra.

TAKE YOUR PULSE: PUT YOUR FINGER ON THE PULSE OF YOUR OPENNESS TO NEGATIVITY

While in general it is always good to be open to different ideas and experiences, in the case of negativity, openness is a bad thing! In this chapter, we will check on just how open you are to the negative influences around you. Answer the following questions using the scale of one to five hearts and see how effectively you have shut yourself against the P4s and other negative traps that can waylay even the most promising of brands and careers. The lower your score, the better off you are.

Scale

5 ♥♥♥♥♥	Strongly agree	That's really, really true about me.
4 ♥♥♥♥	Agree	That would be me.
3 ♥♥♥	Somewhat agree	50/50 sometimes, sometimes not.
2 ♥♥	Disagree	That absolutely has nothing to do with me.
1 ♥	Strongly disagree	Let me take the fifth on this.

What's Your Pulse Rate? 6.5 Questions Measuring How You Deal with Negativity

1. I find myself spending a lot of time worrying about negative things that were said about me.

2. I internalize 40 percent or more of the negative feedback that people say about me.

3. If you want to stop me dead in my tracks, just give me negative feedback.

4. I learn very little from negative feedback.

5. I know how to extract the positive out of negative feedback and use it to strengthen myself.

6. I often elect to do something fun and pleasurable even when I know I should be working on something that will bring me a greater degree of success.

6.5 I crumble very easily under pressure.

Now that you've taken the test, let's analyze your openness to negativity:

Scores

- **29–35:** You are wide open. You are extremely sensitive to the opinions and judgments of others and are constantly second-guessing yourself for fear of doing something that will bring criticism. As long as you carry this self-defeating attitude, you will not be able to build a successful brand or achieve your aspirations. You need to start strengthening your resolve and following the 6.5 steps to omitting negativity before you find your career completely derailed. Remember that negativity can just as easily leave through an open door as it can enter!

- **21–28:** You are easily accessible. You are not completely dominated by negativity in the way a wide-open colleague is, and you probably function in a fairly positive manner if you are not facing any outright negativity. But once negative people and influences appear, you quickly come under their sway. Negativity instinctively senses and pursues its most vulnerable targets, so you probably encounter it often. You also need to review the 6.5 steps and make sure to follow each one thoroughly if you want to have any chance of overcoming negativity to build a successful brand.

- **14–20:** You are behind closed doors. You have managed to remove yourself from the run-of-the-mill negativity that most of us encounter on a regular basis. You do not allow yourself to become snared or distracted by offhand comments and petty political maneuverings. But closed doors are not the same as locked doors. Serious negativity, the type that damages lives and ruins careers if left unchecked, can still open your door and find you. You have taken some good first steps, but do not assume you are now safe. You still have plenty of work to do.

- **9–13:** You are behind a locked door with a peephole. You understand the threat negativity poses and the many different forms it takes and have developed effective strategies to deflect or neutralize it. Your door is locked, making it extremely difficult for negativity to get through. But your door still has a peephole, indicating that you find it hard to resist occasionally glimpsing at negativity and letting it invade your thoughts. Like most things that are bad for us, negativity holds a peculiar attraction. Resist it—there are much better ways to spend your precious spare time than focusing on negativity!

- **7–8:** You are behind a reinforced steel door with a deadbolt lock. You have erected complete defenses against negativity. Your door is impenetrable to the intrusion of negativity, unless you choose to open it. The lack of any type of peephole indicates that you have learned to ignore the dangerous allure of negativity and instead put it completely out of your life. You have truly omitted negativity, bringing you one major step closer to building the best possible brand and achieving all of your aspirations.

IT'S SHOWTIME!: Commit to the constant battle of overcoming negativity, and take daily, weekly, monthly, quarterly, and yearly steps to put your plan into action

Omitting negativity is a constant battle. Once you have successfully overcome a negative challenge, it is not time to relax, because the next negative challenge lurks around the corner. Listed in the chart that follows are ways you can integrate vigilance against negativity into your regular routine without allowing yourself to become consumed by it.

FREQUENCY	WHAT CAN I DO?	HOW DOES IT HELP MY BRAND?
DAILY	Anticipate negative events for that day and develop responses.	Daily anticipation of potential negative events will quickly build an impressive arsenal of effective strategies to combat negativity.
WEEKLY	Conduct a mid-week negativity review and give yourself the power to resolve any negative issues.	Grant yourself the ability to meet and overcome challenges head-on. By reviewing all the negativity you have encountered every week, you can empower yourself to omit it by the most appropriate means—for example, give yourself the power to decline a lunch invitation from the office gossip.
MONTHLY	Conduct a negativity "temperature check."	In a given month, you will encounter numerous negative situations that get you hot under the collar. Select the five most blood-boiling incidents and review them with an eye toward developing new tools to combat and omit them. Bring in your Branding Board of Advisers for some objective outside opinion. In this way you can lower your temperature back to a safe level.

FREQUENCY	WHAT CAN I DO?	HOW DOES IT HELP MY BRAND?
QUARTERLY	Conduct a "lemonade session."	In a "lemonade session," you take negative comments or experiences (lemons) and brainstorm ways to turn them into something positive (lemonade, or if you want to make more money, turn them into lemon polish). Consciously empower yourself to stay positive and professional in the face of negativity and thus avoid damaging your brand. Invite your Branding Board to help you take three lemons and score your efforts to make them lemonade on five factors—professionalism, three-second impression, recognizing the root cause of problem, developing responses that prevent the event from reoccurring, and being passionate about turning the event around.
YEARLY	Clean out your brain's recycle bin.	Your brain is the most powerful computer you will ever use (more on that shortly). Like any computer, your brain collects a lot of trash that needs to be placed in the recycle bin and then emptied. Every year, conduct a thorough mental review of all the negative experiences you had to go through, how you resolved them, and what you learned. Then completely clear whatever brain space the negative events themselves are taking up, while retaining the strategies and lessons you learned.

Text Message

The hardest part of omitting the negative is developing and maintaining the willpower and mental toughness required to truly repel negativity from your life. Most of the actual strategies for omitting negativity (avoiding negative people, ignoring negative comments, etc.) are fairly simple and straightforward. Keeping this spirit of simplicity in mind, compose a 10-second text message that sums up how you will omit the negative from your life and your career.

_____

_____

FRESH TECHNOLOGIES: INCREASE THE COMPUTING POWER OF YOUR BRAIN

Your brain is the most powerful computer you will ever use. You possess more problem-solving capability, creativity, intuition, and reasoning than the entire collection of supercomputers at NASA's disposal. But like any piece of technology, your brain is not intrinsically helpful or harmful. You are both the problem and the solution for your brand-building efforts. It all depends how you deploy the incredible computer sitting between your ears.

You can increase the computing power of your brain even further by doing things like taking classes or otherwise improving your knowledge (adding RAM), following the steps of Fresh PASSION to empower yourself to use all your skills to their maximum capacity (putting in a more powerful motherboard), and regularly reading and staying generally observant and impassioned to keep your mind sharp and engaged so that you can quickly get the grasp of a situation and figure out the best strategy to take advantage of it (increasing the speed of your Internet connection from dial-up to broadband).

To more effectively omit the negative, one of the most powerful computing tools your brain offers is the control/alt/delete command. Namely, you can *control* what you let into your thoughts and affect your actions; *alter* how people perceive you by displaying your passion, skills, and dedication; and *delete* negative people, activities, and experiences from your life. Your brain is the freshest piece of technology available on the market, and it's yours at no cost!

BROWNIE BITE

Visit http://www.MyFreshBrand.com and download a Lemonade Form. This form will help you organize your list of lemons for your quarterly Lemonade Session and then score your responses.

THE DOGGIE BAG: THE OMITTING THE NEGATIVE TAKEAWAYS

1. Negativity is, unfortunately, a guaranteed part of life. Negativity is constantly emanating from the environment around you, including from family, friends, and colleagues who may not even realize that they are being negative. Do not waste your precious time and resources dealing with negativity. Remember, you are building a foundation that will lead to a stellar career with opportunities for enhancement, a thriving business, or a new venture. You simply don't have time to waste. Omitting the negative will be an extremely useful skill that you should carry with you throughout your professional and personal life.

2. When you encounter a negative experience—learn from it. Review the experience in your mind. Where did it come from? Why did it happen? Was it something you should have foreseen or was it out of the blue? What are some warning signs that will alert you to a similar negative experience arising in the future? However, don't spend a lot of time dwelling on the negative experience. You don't need to let it consume valuable real estate in your head; you have so much more ahead of you.

3. In particular, you will have to successfully deal with the dreaded "P4" of negativity—pain, pleasure, pressure, and persecution. On this journey to personal and professional success you will have to

deal with these four major obstacles and your challenge will be to not let any of them derail you. P4s will be potentially negative derailments to your personal and professional success journey. They have a strong potential to have a negative impact, and the way in which you tackle and overcome these potential derailments is critical to your obtaining and sustaining success.

You must go through each aspect of the P4s to learn from them, but don't let them lead you, consume you or cause you to lose focus. You will need to omit these potential negatives both proactively and reactively. Find the lessons that all this negativity can teach you and use them to write the next successful chapter. Do it right and pretty soon you will be experiencing exponential personal, academic and professional success.

4. You will need to fight against negativity, and fight hard, to fully build your brand and achieve your aspirations. But remember that you must fight fair and fight subtly. When you find a knife in your back, the natural inclination is to stick it right between the shoulder blades of the person who stuck it there. Resist the temptation.

5. You can do untold long-lasting damage to your brand and your reputation by acting unprofessionally in the face of negativity. Even if a colleague is behaving unprofessionally toward you, you must be professional and dignified in your response. One of the most insidious aspects of negativity is how easy it is to become drawn in by negativity and become negative yourself. If you cannot actively retaliate against negativity without taking negative actions yourself, your best bet is to ignore it. You will look mature and professional that way, as opposed to a negative person who may be spreading rumors or using other underhanded tricks against you. Trust me, people will soon figure out what is going on without you risking your brand to tell them.

6. You need to create an arsenal of solutions to deal with negative events. Catalogue negative events as they happen, and also try to anticipate negative events that may pop up during the day. Do not dwell on them, but only focus on lessons you can learn and

strategies you can use to combat them. That way when negativity does arise, you will have a ready-made arsenal of tools and processes at your disposal to quickly deal with whatever negative obstacle you are facing.

Grant yourself the ability to meet and overcome challenges head-on. You need to be fully empowered to take whatever appropriate steps are necessary to omit negativity from your career and your life. This can mean allowing yourself to decline to socialize with colleagues who spread rumors or bring down your morale, even if they wind up getting offended. It can also mean giving yourself the power to be the bigger person and walk away from a needless confrontation, or gaining power to advance in your academic and future professional career despite negative opposition by taking courses or developing skills that will serve you much better than engaging in petty office politics. Grant yourself the power to make it right!

6.5 Remember to relax. Negativity is inevitable and potentially poses a serious threat to your brand and career, but by overly worrying about it, you succumb to its pressures. Be vigilant and forceful in your response to negativity, but don't allow that response to consume you. If you properly follow the steps outlined in this chapter, you should be amply prepared to meet and overcome whatever challenges negativity may throw your way. It's hard to be focused and passionate if you are excessively nervous about the obstacles you will face. Don't sweat the negativity too much—with Fresh PASSION on your side you are sure to beat it!

9
Fresh Passion: Nailing the Brand

Quotable Notable: Stephen King

Brownie Point: Yes, True Success Is Possible

Nailing the Brand—The Concept, Rationale, and Importance

6.5 Fresh Steps toward Nailing the Brand

- **Nailing the Brand: Step 1**—Discover your perfect day goal.
- **Nailing the Brand: Step 2**—Create a Fresh 10-second text message.
- **Nailing the Brand: Step 3**—Create a Fresh 30-second Super Bowl commercial.
- **Nailing the Brand: Step 4**—Distill down to your brand statement.
- **Nailing the Brand: Step 5**—Develop a brand logo.
- **Nailing the Brand: Step 6**—Make a business card based on your personal brand and logo.
- **Nailing the Brand: Step 6.5**—Make it Real and Keep it Fresh—Branding is for life.

It's Showtime!: Becoming a brand is a comprehensive process; take daily, weekly, monthly, quarterly, and yearly steps to put your plan into action

Brownie Bite

The Doggie Bag: The Nailing the Brand Takeaways

> *"I am the literary equivalent of a Big Mac and fries."*
>
> —STEPHEN KING

QUOTABLE NOTABLE: STEPHEN KING

Horror/fantasy author Stephen King is one of the most successful writers of all time in any genre, with over 50 bestselling novels to his credit, as well as numerous film and television adaptations of his work. King grew up in poverty in rural Maine and was a struggling schoolteacher when a major publisher accepted his first novel *Carrie* after 26 rejections. King's passion for the craft of writing and invigorated spirit allowed him to keep pursuing his aspiration of becoming a published novelist through this long period of professional struggle and rejection. Focusing on popular themes and aiming his work at mainstream readers looking for entertainment (just as McDonald's aims its Big Mac and fries at the mainstream consumer looking for a quick and fun meal), King has developed himself into a leading literary brand whose fans know what to expect from him, and he has clearly carved out a niche for himself in the brutally competitive publishing marketplace (just as McDonald's has clearly branded itself in the brutally competitive fast-food marketplace).

BROWNIE POINT: YES, TRUE SUCCESS IS POSSIBLE—PART 1

If ever there was a time where I needed to nail my brand, it was during my leadership assignment as a retail operations manger (see the section "If You Thought Presidential Politics Were Tough, Check Out the Office" in the previous chapter). There were many doubters, naysayers, and pessimistic people who thought I would fall flat on my face. I think they knew I had some substance, but they hadn't really experienced the whole package of the Michael D. Brown brand.

I decided to use this "negative event" as a momentum builder and show my new employees and colleagues that their perception of me as having no chance for success was dead wrong. I drew upon the formula that had aided my previous success, Fresh PASSION, to provide the road map forward. What employees of the head office, and of the entire business across the United States, began to experience was a fresh servant/leader who could get things done through and with people.

I spent the first 60 days speaking with the frontline employees and my leadership team. I spent the next 30 days investing in my leadership team members' personal and professional development (this investment continued throughout my tenure). After the first three months, I was able to communicate a passionate vision and strategy with my team on how we would move the business forward and win. Now believing in me and my commitment to them and the business, they agreed to join me on the journey.

By the sixth month in my new management position, the tides had turned for me. The former skeptics and naysayers now wanted to have lunch with me so we could chat about what I was doing to deliver such impressive results. By the end of the first year, many of those who had once been my harshest critics throughout the organization showered me with enormous praise for my performance and leadership.

My boss called me into his office and lauded me with a level of praise that was just astonishing. He thanked me for delivering double-digit growth, ranking number one among my peers in every key performance metric, displaying unwavering professionalism (He had known of the tension in the business around my arrival.), and providing strong leadership. He went on to say that he was impressed with how quickly I had started delivering results and that he had spoken to my leadership team and heard nothing but high praise for me.

This job really internally and externally validated my ability to perform and deliver as a senior-level leader and provided a boost and enhancement to my brand that delivered and continues to deliver tremendous returns and ever-increasing equity. By taking on the challenge of a senior management role relatively early in my career and toughing it through all the negativity I encountered along the way, I obtained a level of personal brand equity that would have otherwise taken me 10 more years to develop. By staying laser-focused on delivering results, I nailed my personal brand, and only good things have happened as a result.

Yes, True Success Is Possible—Part 2

In today's world of global expansion and virtual working environments, you will not always have the opportunity like I had in the previous story to personally show the decision makers your brand. Nor will all the decision makers have the opportunity to experience your brand. That is why it is so critical for you to have a branded package that has strong internal substance, a track record of delivering top-quality results, and a professional appearance that can help decision makers arrive at a strong impression of your ability to provide value to their organization—even if you are not physically in their presence. This is equally true for entrepreneurs, whose "decision makers" are ultimately their customers, whether they directly deal with them or not!

Let me finish the story in the section titled "Layoff Lemons to Leadership Lemonade" in Chapter 7 to give you a prime example of the importance of building a brand so strong and competitive that people you have never met or worked with perceive it in high regard. Do it right and these people are still willing to be an ambassador for you and sell your brand to others.

Remember my boss Bradley who "represented" me during one of the many downsizings I survived? Well, he didn't exactly tell me the entire story of what went on at the downsizing meeting. About a year after taking the engineering role, I was having lunch with a director who had been part of the downsizing discussion where they were deciding who would stay and who would be let go. He told me that when the dust settled, he wanted to tell me about a discussion that had happened a year earlier. I asked him to tell me right then and there, but he insisted the time wasn't right.

Another six months went by and I bumped into him. Once again I asked him to tell me about the discussion; this time he agreed, saying, "Michael, when we were selecting people for the new organization, your boss ranked you very low and said he didn't think you were a good performer. And something happened that I have never seen before: a number of people in the room started rumbling. One person said, 'What do you mean, this guy has delivered in every role that he has been in.' Another person said, 'I don't think we are talking about the same person.' And the positive comments went on and on from people all over the business."

Continuing as a smile slowly began creeping across my face, he said, "Finally, people started saying, 'I will take him in a heartbeat.' And then a debate started among four departments on why you should be assigned to their group. Your boss just stood there with a pretty dumb look on his face." This director said, "Michael, you have made an impact on this entire business and so many people know it, even people for whom you have never worked. Keep doing what you are doing."

Now beaming ear to ear, I realized that I had nailed the brand on the outside and inside; people knew me by my personal brand of getting results through and with people.

I also had permeated the organization and had brand ambassadors advocating on my behalf if and when I wasn't present. They were spreading the word of my value and substance. I later learned that the president of the organization had been my biggest advocate for the senior leadership role that I spoke about in the previous chapter.

I had met the president briefly on about three different occasions in the past, for a total of about 2 hours. My commitment to building my brand via working on cross-functional virtual teams, delivering in my current assignments, assuming additional responsibilities, working on initiatives where the results impacted the entire organization, networking, continuing to stay fresh, and building a track record of consistently delivering results above and beyond the plan had allowed me to cement a reputation as a branded expert who could deliver fresh results.

As far as Bradley is concerned, he and I ended up crossing paths again in a meeting two years after I had moved on to three different roles within the company. He had assumed another role as well. Bradley told me, "When I first became your boss, you and me didn't hit it off well. But I have to say I really respect you for your work ethic, the way you get things done, and your leadership ability. So many people in this organization have such a high opinion of you and are big fans of yours. I am hoping that the little incident we had didn't give you a bad opinion of me. In hindsight I think both of us acted unprofessionally."

There are many critical and cutting things I could have said in response that would have felt really good and also been 100 percent accurate. Instead, I chose to take the high road and omit the negative from both our lives. I simply said, "Bradley, I respect you as a professional," and put the incident permanently behind us.

Remember, you know you have nailed the brand when people who you have never met are advocating for you!

NAILING THE BRAND—THE CONCEPT, RATIONALE, AND IMPORTANCE

After the freshness, preparation, aspiration, selling, staying laser-focused, and omitting the negative have all helped you develop the substance of your powerful brand, land your brand, and given you the tools to be able to successfully sell yourself, it is time to nail, package, and market it to your audience (employer, group, organization).

Answer these questions: Who am I? What do I want to be? How do I want to be perceived? Most of us don't think of ourselves as "a package," but after reading this book you won't make that mistake again. All of us are packages (i.e., "she is so plain; don't depend on him he will never deliver; he is just boring"). Just make sure that you control your packaging (the look, feel, and experience) and the message that illuminates from it.

Honestly, how many times have you bought something just because of the packaging, or paid more for something because it was presented in an exciting way? That's the main reason we want to pay less for generic—the packaging is uniformly dull. When we see a package that shouts "Energy, Invigoration, Crisp, Clean, Colorful, Beautiful, Sophisticated, Expensive," we are willing to pay more.

In essence, good packaging helps *speed the purchasing decision* and leads people to *pay top dollar* (and that's what you want your packaging to do, right?). Packaging is how you express your personality. So think about how you want to be perceived and what competitive edge you want your packaging to show. What does your package need to look like and feel like in order for you to become recognized as a leader at your company by colleagues as well as management? Or to get the employer to pay you $120K? Or to get customers to knock the door down to get to your products and services?

The way you decide to package your unique brand should be evident in everything that you do and attach your name to, the way you walk, the way you talk, the way you dress, the content and appearance of your resume/cover letter, your award-winning interview. Think about globally dominant brands like Starbucks and Coca-Cola. Those brands offer a whole experience, a whole way of life, which is instantly conjured in your mind when you hear about or see them. That does not happen by accident.

Speaking of packaging, another globally dominant brand comes to mind: Godiva chocolate. Godiva is one of the most respected brands of chocolate on the market. If you want to impress or send a strong message, you are likely to buy Godiva. The purchaser knows the brand substance (i.e., the chocolate itself) from what they have heard through raving reviews of people who have tasted the chocolate. However, a key driver, and in many cases the main driver, that accelerates the buyer to make a purchase decision is the packaging.

No doubt Godiva knows this and therefore expends a great deal of research and money in presenting a package that is attractive, competitive, fresh, striking, and delivers a world-class experience on first sight (within three seconds). Oh, by the way, this packaging also commands a lot more money than the packaging of Godiva's competitors, even other luxury chocolate brands. This is what you personally want to do with your own brand. You want to be so competitive that you are rewarded at a far greater rate/level than your competitor (who may be a coworker, buddy, another business, etc.) who may offer similar talents and services.

So that's what "Nailing the Brand" is—it's successfully packaging yourself. You have spent some fantastic time with me reading this great book that served to help you build and present your solid, fresh, and competitive substance via preparation, aspiration, staying laser-focused, selling your value, invigoration, and omitting the negative. Now here is the final and most crucial part.

Most people—future employers, existing employers, companies, organizations, etc.—will not get the opportunity to experience your substance if your outside packaging does not scream: "Passionate, excited, fresh, filled with integrity, competitive, skilled, and determined." So nailing the brand is about packaging your substance (your core) and putting a bow on it so that you become a fresh brand that can successfully compete and WIN internally and externally, which will enable you to achieve exponential personal and professional success.

Your core substance remains who you are—you will add, enhance, and keep it fresh to be competitive. The stronger your brand's return on investment (ROI) and equity, the greater the return to your pocket. In order for your brand to work, it must reflect your core substance.

For example, if you have a true passion and knack for marketing and have spent years building an impressive portfolio, this is what you should base your brand on. You may enhance your brand as a marketer by doing things like obtaining advanced degrees and becoming fluent in all the latest Internet-based marketing concepts like Search Engine Optimization (SEO), but you are still building on your marketing core.

If you suddenly try to brand yourself as a professional photographer and pour all your time and money into developing a photography portfolio, you will most likely fail. This is not to say you shouldn't pursue photography as a personal hobby, or even learn the basics to help you with visual presentation in your marketing efforts. Totally shifting gears to an area where you have not previously displayed any great talent is not advisable. The marketplace has an uncanny ability to detect brands that are phony or off the mark.

Therefore, an important part of nailing the brand is knowing yourself. You can tap into your passion and figure out what you are good at (remember the earlier you identify your passion, connect it to your brand and deliver, the greater your chances for achieving exponential personal and professional success).

Let's look at a couple of examples of how getting away from your core substance in your branding efforts can cause major problems. We will use two of the companies we previously mentioned as generally successful in their brand-building efforts: Coca-Cola and Starbucks.

Depending on your age, you may remember the huge branding debacle that was known as "New Coke." In 1985, Coca-Cola, one of the world's most recognized and successful brands, changed the formula of its signature beverage to meet what the company thought was growing consumer preference for a sweeter cola. Coke drinkers everywhere were outraged, sales sharply declined, and three months later, Coca-Cola reintroduced the original formula.

After reintroducing the original brand under the name "Coca-Cola Classic," Coca-Cola President Donald Keough publicly stated, "The simple fact is that all the time and money and skill poured into consumer research on the new Coca-Cola could not measure or reveal the deep and abiding emotional attachment to original Coca-Cola felt by so many people."[4]

There is little I can add to Mr. Keough's excellent summary of how a truly great brand inspires deep emotional attachment that will sustain it through petty fluctuations in popular tastes. That is the type of brand you want to build, and you can only do so by remaining true to yourself.

More recently, coffee chain Starbucks decided to discontinue selling warm breakfast sandwiches. These sandwiches, normally more associated with doughnut shops than with upscale cafes, interfered with Starbucks' brand presentation as the "third place" between home and work where professional people can relax with a cup of premium coffee, listen to relaxing background music, and perhaps wirelessly surf the Internet on their laptop computers.

"In short, the scent of the warm sandwiches interferes with the coffee aroma in our stores," Starbucks Chairman and Chief Executive Howard D. Schultz was quoted as saying in a Jan. 31, 2008 *New York Times* article.[5] In an earlier leaked corporate memo, Schultz wrote, "We have had

---

4. "It's the Anniversary of the Day Coca-Cola Will Never Forget," *Soda Pop Dreams*, Spring 2005, http://www.sodaspectrum.com/36_newcoke.htm.

5. Andrew Martin, "Starbucks to Close Stores and End Sandwich Sales," *New York Times*, Jan. 31, 2008, http://www.nytimes.com/2008/01/31/business/31sbux.html.

to make a series of decisions that, in retrospect, have led to the watering down of the Starbucks experience, and what some might call the commoditization of our brand."[6] Like Coca-Cola, Starbucks tried tinkering with its brand essence in order to respond to what it perceived as a shift in the marketplace, without really considering the long-term implications for its established brand. Starbucks even closed almost 1,000 stores in the United States during 2008 and 2009. Who ever thought we'd see the day that Starbucks would be closing stores?

Rather than making brand-appropriate modifications, such as introducing a new line of designer coffee or new scone flavors, Starbucks defied its own careful brand-building efforts by selling the same kind of "on the go" snack you would find at a fast-food restaurant. It's amazing how a seemingly minor decision like offering warm breakfast sandwiches can quickly snowball into a major brand catastrophe.

No brand can be all things to all people, and some customers will always prefer a different brand experience than the one you offer. As long as you nail your brand, though, you will attract the kind of loyal, repeat business that turns brands like Coca-Cola and Starbucks into global icons.

Consider that Coca-Cola and Starbucks employ some of the best, most highly paid branding experts out there, and they still made major errors in their branding efforts. If Coke can screw up, so can you! Always be vigilant about how you are presenting yourself in the marketplace and how closely the brand you present matches the experience and value you deliver.

Furthermore, it is absolutely a must that your brand be evident in and on everything that your name is attached to (this is the whole package). For example, you can't say that your brand represents professionalism and then have your marketing material (business card, portfolio, resume, last project presentation) look as though the printer ran out of ink and the paper has a sampling of your breakfast spilled on it. You can't say that you are someone whose brand is one that can take on complex responsibilities when you are late to work every day.

---

6. "Starbucks exec calls brand diluted," *San Diego Union Tribune*, Feb. 24, 2007, http://www.signonsandiego.com/uniontrib/20070224/news_1b24starbuck.html.

This is the whole package that encapsulates everything and puts into perspective what people will see and experience from you. Improperly executed, packaging becomes a barrier. People won't want to try your brand if the impression is wrong. The best "skilled" people don't always get the job. A competitor with lesser skills who has done a better job of packaging herself and presenting a coherent, appealing brand could easily beat you out for a job, promotion, or leadership opportunity. Put the necessary effort into developing a professional network, image, and reputation now, and you will have much better future success in winning the promotions, jobs, and clients you desire.

That said, behind the presentation there does need to be solid substance. People need good reason to subscribe to your brand. This requires creating trust and belief to get them in and nail your brand even further. Don't be an "empty suit"—looking great at first glance but offering nothing but fluff beyond that. An empty suit may open some doors and even be offered some opportunities, but at some point that empty suit will collapse upon itself. Hot air only takes you so far!

Ultimately, nailing the brand is like following through on a baseball swing. You could have a textbook-perfect batting stance and swing mechanics that would make Ted Williams drool, but if you wimp out once you connect with the ball instead of following the swing all the way through, you will hit a pop fly instead of a home run. Likewise, you could devote years of effort toward developing all the skills and capabilities you could ever need to deliver premium value in your chosen field of branded expertise. But if you skimp on how you package yourself, you will only obtain generic results instead of becoming a market leader and achieving your aspirations.

6.5 FRESH STEPS TOWARD NAILING THE BRAND

- *Nailing the Brand: Step 1*
  Discover your perfect day goal.
- *Nailing the Brand: Step 2*
  Create a Fresh 10-second text message.

- *Nailing the Brand: Step 3*
  Create a Fresh 30-second Super Bowl commercial.
- *Nailing the Brand: Step 4*
  Distill down to your brand statement.
- *Nailing the Brand: Step 5*
  Develop a brand logo.
- *Nailing the Brand: Step 6*
  Make a business card based on your personal brand and logo.
- *Nailing the Brand: Step 6.5*
  Make it Real and Keep it Fresh—Branding is for life.

Let's package all that you have learned from this journey via this book. Go back to the worksheets you filled out in earlier chapters and duplicate what you filled out in the following pages, so that you have all your branding exercises and tools in one spot.

Don't feel obligated to "duplicate" anything too closely—it is entirely possible your viewpoint on your brand has changed or deepened as a result of what you have learned in your subsequent readings. Feel free to make any changes necessary to reflect your most current brand strategy and aspirations. Also hold on to this Success Package and continue to update it in the months and years ahead as you continue to grow and go through brand-building experiences, so that your brand grows with you!

Nailing the Brand: Step 1—Discover your perfect day goal

> **Write Your PERFECT DAY Five Years From Now**

This is a day where you can wake up and say, "Wow, I have achieved my desired personal and professional success and I am going to keep going and do even better!" If you are like me you just might want to type this out instead of handwriting it (I am still learning how to read my own handwriting).

Now let's get started, and don't leave out any of the small details. Be sure to think as large and as globally as you like. Here are some questions to consider and answer: What does your family look like? What's your financial picture? What are you doing professionally? What does your personal life look like? What does personal and professional success look like? Are you an entrepreneur? Are you working in a corporation? Are you employed inside your home? Where do you vacation? Do you own real estate? Do you have a favorite cause/charity that you are giving back to? What are your credentials?

_____

_____

_____

_____

_____

_____

_____

_____

_____

_____

_____

fresh PASSION: Nailing the Brand

You can download this form at www.MyFreshBrand.com

Michael D. Brown's Perfect Day Five Years From Now

- I am debt free using the earnings of my investments to support and finance my foundation, the Fresh Results Institute, business, and further personal, professional growth/goals.

- I am staying fresh with specialty and advanced training, certifications, and credentialing in my area of branded expertise.

- God is still the center and is still working through me.

- My personal and professional success continues to accelerate and stay fresh—I'm forever growing both personally and professionally.

- I am fully engaged in my personal and professional success and in total alignment: physically, mentally, emotionally, and spiritually.

- I am speaking for Fortune 500 companies and business schools.

- My daily investment fee for clients has increased 55 percent and I am delivering 55 percent more return on their investment.

- I am delivering and driving fresh results through and with people while offering a unique experience. My work is underpinned by my Fresh Customer Service and Fresh PASSION tools and processes. My main focus here is to help individuals, organizations, and companies achieve exponential personal, professional, and economic growth. This work has a coaching, speaking, training, and seminar component. I have completed the books on Fresh Customer Service (done!) and Fresh PASSION (you are reading it now).

- This feels really good, because I am working in my destiny and doing what I am passionate about and I am making a difference in the lives of individuals and in organizations.

- I have opened the Fresh Results Institute—serving over 1,000 people.

- I have a Ritz-Carlton vacation home in Florida.
- I have a slate of products centered around Fresh Customer Service and Fresh PASSION. This includes books, manuals, audio, teleseminars, online courses, and other training materials.
- My personal relationship has been strengthened with my family—I am spending the holidays with them and I am taking them on an all-expenses-paid vacation once a year
- My health is in tip-top shape, and I am still working out.
- I have started the Michael D. Brown Foundation that's investing in communities around the country with a special focus on helping young people with their communication skills, and removing the blockages that are preventing people from achieving exponential personal, professional, and economic success.

***Nailing the Brand: Step 2*—Create a Fresh 10-second text message**

Write your Fresh 10-second text message

This should be quick, filled with impact, powerful, clear, and compelling.

_____

_____

_____

***Nailing the Brand: Step 3*—Create a Fresh 30-second Super Bowl commercial**

Write your Fresh 30-second Super Bowl commercial

_____

_____

_____

_____

_____

_____

***Nailing the Brand: Step 4*—Distill down to your brand statement**

Write your brand statement

_____

_____

_____

Nailing the Brand: Step 5—Develop a brand logo

Sketch out a logo that represents your brand

If you had to describe this logo to someone in 10 seconds, what would you say?

_____

_____

_____

In the conclusion of the book you will see the story behind my logo that is on the cover of this book.

***Nailing the Brand: Step 6*—Make a business card based on your personal brand and logo**

Create your new business card

Include your logo and your brand statement.

You can see my business card @ www.MyFreshBrand.com.

Nailing the Brand: Step 6.5—Make it Real and Keep it Fresh—Branding is for life

> *"Your newly found brand is the product of your intelligent decision. You must keep the brand fresh, competitive, nurtured and loved!"*
>
> —MICHAEL D. BROWN

So you made it through all the steps of Fresh PASSION. Congratulations! Your new and/or enhanced brand will make you a highly competitive branded expert who can provide any company, individual, customer, or organization a substantial return for their investment in you. This will lead to an increase in your brand recognition and brand equity. You have the key ingredients (great return on investment, brand equity, and recognition) so that you will be rewarded at a much greater level and experience exponential personal, academic, and professional success.

When your brand is fresh and highly competitive, you will be viewed as a branded expert and asset both internally and on the open market (especially to potential employers or customers). This will lead to more people, organizations, and/or companies subscribing to what you have to offer while providing you with a great, competitive, and substantial return (i.e., more money, more opportunities for personal and professional growth, more customers, etc.).

When your brand is stale and not up for the challenge posed by the many other quality brands on the market, you will most likely die generic—meaning you will linger on the shelf and be passed over for brands that are more established in the marketplace and more attractively packaged.

Your newly minted and/or enhanced brand will greatly aid, influence, and enable you to experience exponential personal and professional success today, tomorrow, and well into the future. You are now armed, tooled, and better positioned to experience your perfect day much sooner than you could have ever imagined.

To put it another way, imagine taking the core and substance of the ideas from each chapter and putting them all together—this is the bow that wraps around your brand, not unlike the bow wrapping a box of Godiva chocolates. It's an overarching thing that in large part both holds your brand together and also presents it to the outside world. How strong is your bow, and how enticing does it look?

Remember that enacting and achieving Fresh PASSION is a lifetime journey. From time to time, you need to go back and untie your bow to make sure it is still fresh and competitive. Don't be afraid to retie it in a new, tighter knot, or even to replace it with a new bow entirely if you need to!

Accelerate yourself far beyond the zone of a convenient generic and jump into the zone of being a fresh and competitive brand that will yield exponential personal and professional success. Remember that you must take the space and own it, don't wait or expect someone to give you a parcel of land or a parcel of opportunity. Figure out the space you want to operate in and go for it.

The danger in waiting for someone to loan you the space or give you the space puts you in a landlord-tenant relationship and subjects you to an anytime eviction. This eviction is the equivalent of a generic death, meaning your brand is not strong enough to create the buzz among consumers that is needed to guarantee you prime shelf space. When you create a competitive brand, you get to pick the prime lots and will be rewarded with the opportunity to stay (and be rewarded greatly) because your outputs are too valuable to evict. Instead you get to stay fresh and competitive so you are in charge of your destiny, whether internally or on the open marketplace. A competitive brand that is kept fresh and connected to your passion is unbeatable.

To put it another way, find the fertile ground and sow your brand upon it and reap the harvest. Branded seeds germinate personal and professional success with a faster and more bountiful harvest than generic seeds.

IT'S SHOWTIME!: BECOMING A BRAND IS A COMPREHENSIVE PROCESS; TAKE DAILY, WEEKLY, MONTHLY, QUARTERLY, AND YEARLY STEPS TO PUT YOUR PLAN INTO ACTION

Over the previous seven chapters, you have accumulated quite a few daily, weekly, quarterly, monthly, and yearly tasks. To help you remember them all and prioritize them, in the following pages we have provided you with a comprehensive view of all the daily, weekly, quarterly, monthly, and yearly charts. You can now put a Y for yes or an N for no on the completed column. Feel free to add notes in the notes as well. This is your moment to take action that will put you on the path to making this a reality and achieve personal and professional success. Remember you are the problem and the solution to your success. Remember this is yours, so don't be afraid to decide for yourself exactly how you will accomplish each task and what it will mean to you!

DAILY

WHAT CAN I DO?	HOW DOES IT HELP MY BRAND?	COMPLETED? (Y/N)
Regularly check the RSS feeds you have selected to keep you informed about your area of brand expertise. Also be on constant lookout for new feeds to add.	RSS feeds are the simplest and best way to stay current with the constantly changing flow of information about your area of brand expertise. Remember, information is power!	
Stay informed about current events by reading a newspaper, listening to a radio news broadcast, and/or watching a major television news broadcast.	Keeping up with general current events allows you to learn about larger trends, ideas, and happenings that may have direct or indirect relevance to your specific brand niche. You will also learn about what's going on in the broader economy to understand what obstacles are being faced and how your brand can help solve these obstacles. Also as an informed person you will be a more interesting conversationalist and have more success at networking.	
Read your aspiration notes that you have left around your home, vehicle, and workplace. Don't skip any of them or simply glance—actually read them.	Without daily attention, your aspiration reminder notes will simply become another piece of background clutter you ignore as you focus all your energies on fulfilling short-term minor goals. Force yourself to read each note every day, and take a little time to think about what your aspiration means. This will keep it fresh in your thoughts and make the notes worthwhile.	

WHAT CAN I DO?	HOW DOES IT HELP MY BRAND?	COMPLETED? (Y/N)
Review your daily focus list of goals, objectives, tasks, and responsibilities that must be met to keep you on the path toward your aspiration.	Maintaining and following a daily checklist keeps your mind sharp and your aspiration at the front of your thoughts. It is all too easy to have a "down day"; this will help you avoid having one!	
Hear your 30-second Super Bowl commercial out loud—either affirm it to yourself or actually use it in the field.	You need to constantly hear your commercial to make sure you can deliver it with natural ease and that the contents remain fresh and aligned with your aspirations and your capabilities. If you don't have an opportunity to sell your brand to anyone, try selling it to yourself—it's good practice!	
Take a step "outside the zone" and do something good for yourself or a friend, family member, or colleague.	Spending a few minutes a day treating yourself or someone close to you right will boost your self-esteem and confidence, which in turn will fuel your vigor. Surprise a co-worker with a healthy treat, or carve out time in the day to read a chapter of a favorite novel.	
Anticipate negative events for that day and develop an arsenal of responses.	Your arsenal should be a set of constantly expanding processes and tools you can draw upon when you encounter a problem. Daily anticipation will quickly build an impressive What If Arsenal of effective strategies to combat negativity.	

WEEKLY

WHAT CAN I DO?	HOW DOES IT HELP MY BRAND?	COMPLETED? (Y/N)
Read a well-respected blog by an expert in your area of brand expertise.	Blogs have become an important uncensored form of peer criticism and networking. You will often find out about the "real" happenings in blogs that more formal news sources will not mention.	
Perform a MISS review—examine how effectively you are preparing the mindset, image, skills, and substance portions of your brand.	MISS is not a one-time gut check. It is a constant reevaluation of how your thought process, the way you present yourself, skill set, and overall personal substance are helping or hindering your efforts at success. Weekly checkups will ensure that if you slip in any one of these areas, you will catch it and can rectify the situation before it becomes dire.	
Find an example of someone who made their aspirations come true in a newspaper, magazine, website, or television broadcast. Study how they identified their aspiration and made it happen.	People are making their aspirations come true all the time. By studying a new real-life example every week, you will refresh your passion and determination, and also gain new ideas that may help you in your own pursuits.	
Visit your "focus sanctuary."	Your focus sanctuary is an activity, task, or place you can turn for peace and clarity. At least once a week you should take a little time to pursue a hobby or interest, or visit a favorite secluded spot, to clear your mind of stress and distractions so that you can refocus even stronger and sharper when you return.	

WHAT CAN I DO?	HOW DOES IT HELP MY BRAND?	COMPLETED? (Y/N)
Identify well-known speakers with brands or skills that can help you reach your aspiration and spend an hour either listening to one of their tapes and/or watching one of their videos.	You should constantly energize yourself and obtain fresh ideas and outlooks by seeking out the experiences of people who have already achieved success in your branded field of expertise. While many motivational tapes and videos are less than stellar, there are many good ones, too. Do careful product research to make sure you are only spending time getting quality information from proven successes.	
Have a brief cheerleading session.	Get in touch with your personal and professional success cheerleader to obtain a few "rah rahs." This can be accomplished via text message, email, or other virtual link, as well as by phone or in person. Something as simple as an inspirational email message listing three easy steps you can take to get closer to reaching your aspiration can provide a huge dose of vigor.	
Conduct a mid-week negativity review and give yourself the power to resolve any negative issues.	Grant yourself the ability to meet and overcome challenges head-on. By reviewing all the negativity you have encountered every week, you can empower yourself to omit it by the most appropriate means—for example, give yourself the power to decline a lunch invitation from the office gossip.	

MONTHLY

WHAT CAN I DO?	HOW DOES IT HELP MY BRAND?	COMPLETED? (Y/N)
Attend a meeting of a professional association to which you belong. Actively participate: speak on issues, volunteer for committees and activities, run for elective positions. Also add one person to your network.	Associations are a great networking tool and provide opportunity to gain valuable experience. For example, being treasurer of a group is valid financial management experience you can put on your resume!	
Perform a market check—review the latest job openings, success stories, failures, news, and events in your branded area of expertise. Also speak with one member of your Branding Board of Advisers. For example, a large part of my brand expertise is helping retailers achieve double-digit growth to their bottom line. So I follow a number of retail trade publications to stay abreast of the trends and strategies that are being employed by the competition.	The marketplace is moving faster than ever, thanks to the Internet and other technologies. Jobs open and are filled quickly, new people succeed in new ways while established people grow stale and fall by the wayside, and today's hot skill is tomorrow's useless bit of knowledge. Monthly market checks will help you ensure you are taking preparatory steps that match the current needs of the marketplace.	

WHAT CAN I DO?	HOW DOES IT HELP MY BRAND?	COMPLETED? (Y/N)
Review your progress on reaching your aspirations with one member of your Branding Board of Advisers.	Submitting your aspirations for review by your Branding Board is a critical step, but you need to continually engage them in your aspirations to gain the maximum benefit. Discuss the things you are doing to reach your aspirations with a board member and solicit honest feedback and criticism—this will keep your efforts fresh and allow you to quickly identify and rectify errors and missteps on your part.	
Conduct a focus review with a family member, colleague, or Branding Board member.	Beyond informing the important people in your life about your focus and aspiration, you should actively solicit feedback from them. Conduct a monthly "focus review" where one of these people provides honest input and criticism of how well you are maintaining your focus and minimizing distractions. Use this feedback to make any needed changes or improvements in your focus approach.	

WHAT CAN I DO?	HOW DOES IT HELP MY BRAND?	COMPLETED? (Y/N)
Give a sample pitch of your 30-second Super Bowl commercial to one Branding Board member and one person you would like to influence (a boss, potential employer, new network member, etc.). Solicit constructive feedback and use it to refine your message.	Beyond your daily affirmation/field testing of your commercial, you also need to rehearse it with an audience qualified to provide you with constructive criticism. This will help ensure your commercial is "real world" ready.	
Allow yourself an agenda-less day.	Pick a weekend day, holiday, or vacation day where you will wake up with no concrete goals or plans other than enjoying the day. Free flow it, and don't be afraid to "waste" time doing things like people-watching or window-shopping. When you return to your agenda the following day, you will have enough vigor to complete it twice.	
Conduct a negativity "temperature check."	In a given month, you will encounter numerous negative situations that get you hot under the collar. Select the five most blood-boiling incidents and review them with an eye toward developing new tools for your arsenal and expanding your power to omit them. Bring in your Branding Board of Advisers for some objective outside opinion. In this way you can lower your temperature back to a safe level.	

QUARTERLY

WHAT CAN I DO?	HOW DOES IT HELP MY BRAND?	COMPLETED? (Y/N)
Meet with three to five members of your network, either in person or virtually.	Networking is one skill you must keep honed; unless you regularly stay in contact with your network, your networking skills will grow rusty and your network will erode along with them.	
Arrange a meeting of your Branding Board of Advisers, either virtually or in person.	By bringing your entire Branding Board of Advisers together for a frank quarterly discussion, you can discover where the different aspects of your preparation are in sync and where they may be out of joint. This also allows you to see where you can help your board members!	
Obtain one new skill that will help you reach your aspiration.	No matter how skilled you are, you can always expand your skill set in ways that will bring you even closer to your aspiration. This could involve taking a course, earning a certificate or degree, undergoing on-the-job training or professional development, or even conducting personal research. The key is to keep your career skills fresh, updated, and vital.	

WHAT CAN I DO?	HOW DOES IT HELP MY BRAND?	COMPLETED? (Y/N)
Identify and eliminate one major distraction.	Ignoring distractions is easier than eliminating them, but at least once per quarter you should permanently remove one distraction from your life. This could mean ending contact with someone who is a bad influence, leaving a job that is not helping you reach your aspiration, or ceasing an activity that does not relate to your aspiration.	
Perform an internal "sales review."	You should regard selling your brand in the same way you would regard selling any other high-quality product. Conduct a sales review with yourself, mentally reviewing how many times you pitched your brand, how often you were successful, and what kind of results you achieved. Set quarterly goals and give yourself a bonus if you exceed them. You can also include Branding Board members to get a more thorough review session.	

WHAT CAN I DO?	HOW DOES IT HELP MY BRAND?	COMPLETED? (Y/N)
Administer an emergency booster shot.	Your emergency booster shot can basically be anything that is positive, enjoyable, and allows you to take a short break from your brand without becoming a distraction or obstacle. You can administer these shots "as needed," but you should take one at least once a quarter, even if you're feeling healthy! You will be surprised how much more energetic and excited you are about your brand after spending a little time apart from it!	
Conduct a "lemonade session."	In a "lemonade session," you take negative comments or experiences (lemons) and brainstorm ways to turn them into something positive (lemonade, or if you want to make more money—lemon polish). Consciously empower yourself to stay positive and professional in the face of negativity and thus avoid damaging your brand. Invite your Branding Board to help you take three lemons and score your efforts to make them lemonade on five factors—professionalism, three-second impression, recognizing the root cause of problem, developing responses that prevent the event from reoccurring, and being passionate about turning the event around.	

YEARLY

WHAT CAN I DO?	HOW DOES IT HELP MY BRAND?	COMPLETED? (Y/N)
Evaluate and refresh your network.	Evaluating and refreshing your network allows you to prune members that no longer provide value, renew contact with members who can provide value, and it paves the way to add new members who bring previously unavailable value.	
Thoroughly review everything you have done in the past year to prepare yourself for success. Make at least one major change to your efforts and identify one right move to build on in the coming year. Also evaluate and refresh your Branding Board of Advisers.	Preparation is a critical component of your career performance, so like your overall career performance, it deserves an annual review. You will undoubtedly discover at least one area where a major change is in order and hopefully will identify at least one success you can expand on in future preparatory efforts. Like your larger network, your Branding Board of Advisers needs an annual fine-tuning to make sure every member is the best person possible to help you succeed in a particular area of your brand.	
Carefully review your stated vision of a perfect day and see if it still matches your ideal. Make any changes to your perfect day that are necessary to reflect your current state of mind and then alter your aspiration as needed to fill in any gaps.	Your idea of a perfect day will likely change as your life changes. What may seem ideal one year could seem trivial the next. A yearly review will help keep both your perfect day and your aspiration fresh and in line with your heart's true desires.	

WHAT CAN I DO?	HOW DOES IT HELP MY BRAND?	COMPLETED? (Y/N)
Have a conference call with yourself.	At the very minimum, you should have an annual conference call with yourself where you schedule some "me time" to mentally review your aspiration and the things you do to stay laser-focused on it. Don't be afraid to make some changes based on this "conversation"!	
Set goals at an internal "sales meeting."	Conduct a full-fledged internal sales meeting where you review your performance from the entire previous year, assess strengths and weaknesses, and set goals for the upcoming year. Include perks and bonuses for exceptional performance. You can also include input from Branding Board members here if you wish.	
Allow yourself an agenda-less week.	Everyone deserves a vacation! Take one week out of the year and forget about your brand. Whether you travel to a foreign country, never leave your backyard, or go somewhere in between, pursue fun activities and loosen up a little. When you return, you should have enough spare vigor to carry you through the next year!	

WHAT CAN I DO?	HOW DOES IT HELP MY BRAND?	COMPLETED? (Y/N)
Clean out your brain's recycle bin.	Your brain is the most powerful computer you will ever use. Like any computer, your brain collects a lot of trash that needs to be placed in the recycle bin and then emptied. Every year, conduct a thorough mental review of all the negative experiences you had to go through, how you resolved them, and what you learned. Then completely clear whatever brain space the negative events themselves are taking up, while retaining the strategies and lessons you learned.	

Here is a self-accountability tool

Select a favorite charity to which you would like to donate.

Each time you miss *any* portion of the goals/objectives/tasks on the monthly timeline, put $10 in your charity jar. Donate it every quarter to your selected charity.

Each time you completely achieve the goals/objectives/tasks on the monthly timeline, put $5 in your "Made it Happen" jar. Use these funds to reward yourself!

BROWNIE BITE

The Daily, Weekly, Monthly, Quarterly, and Yearly forms, as well as the perfect day form, are available at www.MyFreshBrand.com. Download as many as you need.

THE DOGGIE BAG: THE NAILING THE BRAND TAKEAWAYS

1. Nailing the brand is all about packaging, or how you present yourself to the outside world. Even the world's most successful brands have failed when they were not properly presented to their customers, or were presented in a way that did not truly represent their core value. The two most important things to remember about packaging yourself is that your packaging is neat, clean, and professional, and that it accurately represents the core value you deliver.

2. Nailing the brand is like following through when you swing a baseball bat. You could have a textbook pure stance and swing that would make Ted Williams drool, but if at the end of that swing you simply tail off instead of finishing with a small follow-through, you will only hit a pop fly instead of a home run. Likewise, you could painstakingly develop your skill set and your professional network to the point where you have a genuinely powerful brand, but if you fail to put the proper effort into how you package that brand, you will find yourself passed by in favor of competitors who may be less qualified but better packaged.

3. Always remember, you only have three seconds to make a first impression, and once that three-second first impression is made, it's an uphill battle to change it, and this is not the position you want to be in, especially if that initial impression was negative. Humans are extremely judgmental by nature, and by nailing the brand, you ensure that the initial judgments passed on you will be positive. Is your brand (and by extension, you personally)

presented in a way that would create an immediate positive impression on a highly qualified professional observer? If not, you need to go back and nail your brand!

4. In many cases, nailing the brand will require spending a significant amount of time and effort fighting against corporate politics, jealousy, and general negativity. Success often breeds resentment, and it is nearly impossible to make a good first impression with someone who holds a personal or professional grudge as a result of your career advancement. The best way to overcome politics and pettiness is to remain above the fray, stay positive, and always treat everyone with professionalism and courtesy, regardless of how they treat you. This may require a great deal of patience, but your brand will come out stronger and shinier than ever.

5. Good packaging speeds the purchasing decision. This is as true in your career as it is on the supermarket shelf. By nailing your brand and packaging yourself as attractively as possible, you will make it easier for prospective employers to decide to hire you, or for prospective clients to engage your services. Easy decisions are fast decisions, and you don't want to wait any longer than necessary to achieve your aspirations and make your perfect day a reality!

6. Your packaging extends to everything you say and do. Dressing neatly and effectively communicating (verbally and non-verbally) are important features of your package, but they are not enough. No matter how impressive your personal appearance and comportment, if you are someone who is chronically late, or is always forgetting to bring a notebook, or constantly offers excuses instead of accomplishing tasks, this negative feature will become part of your brand and part of your package. A successful package accurately represents the core value of the brand inside. A great-looking package may be able to partially hide a flawed brand, but the truth will always come out.

6.5 You will know you have successfully nailed your brand when people you have never met are advocating for you. Truly outstanding brands are rare, so people hear about them and remember them. You may not drink coffee and have never ventured inside a Starbucks in your life, but if I asked you to sum up the Starbucks brand you could probably at least tell me they are an upscale coffee retailer. Also think about how passionately people will defend their favorite politicians or celebrities, based strictly on what they have seen and heard in the media.

If your professional brand is strong enough, people who haven't met you will know about and believe in your reputation, and even be willing to defend it and recommend you (which can be crucial in moving the purchaser who has never met you but who could award you with opportunities, finance, etc.). Now that's brand power!

Final Thoughts: The Last Bite of the Brownie

Quotable Notable: Pablo Picasso

A Challenge: A Final Lesson from My Own Life

6.5 Final Bites

> *"My mother said to me, 'If you are a soldier, you will become a general. If you are a monk, you will become the Pope.' Instead, I was a painter, and became Picasso."*
>
> —PABLO PICASSO (1881–1973)

QUOTABLE NOTABLE: PABLO PICASSO

Spanish painter and sculptor Pablo Picasso is one of the world's best-known and most successful artists. As one of the founders of Cubism, an abstract style of painting that was revolutionary in its time, Picasso withstood intense early criticism and condemnation of his art and continued to develop his unique signature style. Committed to freshness in his work and completely passionate about achieving his aspiration to become a great artist, Picasso disregarded all the negative feedback he received, and in time became renowned as one of the world's most influential painters. Picasso lived a vigorous professional and personal life until his death at age 91, and since that time, he has only grown in stature and reputation in the art world. His name is synonymous with abstract art, and Picasso is the ultimate example of what you can accomplish by staying true to your principles, believing in your individual talents, and refusing to compromise your professional integrity.

A CHALLENGE: A FINAL LESSON FROM MY OWN LIFE

I have to share one more thing with you. I have carried this voice in my head for the many, many years since I graduated high school. A statement was made to me by my elementary school principal, who had moved up to the assistant high school principal by the time I reached high school. His name was Mr. Benny Montgomery.

A few days before high school graduation he said, "Michael, you have every bit of what it takes to succeed. If you fail it is only because of you." For the rest of the day I could hear his voice in my head. And even now some decades later, I can still hear his voice and the high expectations that he set for me. His profound statement gave me the confidence and the belief that I am responsible for my personal and professional success.

I will now present you with a challenge similar to what Mr. Montgomery gave me: You are the problem and solution to your success. Follow the precepts of Fresh PASSION and you will not fail; you will achieve exponential personal and professional success. Go ahead, unleash the Picasso budding inside you, and build your brand while the bottom line builds itself and your aspirations come closer and closer to being met. Picasso was a painter and became Picasso; what will *you* do to become the most personally and professionally successful version of yourself possible and make your perfect day a reality?

6.5 FINAL BITES

You have just consumed an enormous amount of information, far too much to adequately digest in just one sitting. The idea behind this book is not for you to read it once and forget about it. Rather, *Fresh PASSION* is intended to be a workbook, a compass, a road map, an action plan, and a success guide for your daily life that you can refer to on a regular basis. As you advance in your personal and professional life and develop new skills and capabilities that increase your brand appeal, I encourage you to go back and update the worksheet exercises such as describing your perfect day or creating your Super Bowl commercial.

In the spirit of using this book as a working document, I'd also like to caution you not to expect to fully enact Fresh PASSION all at once. It will take time and effort to complete all the steps and work all the concepts and strategies into your life. And of course you are never fully done, since part of Fresh PASSION is always setting new goals once your previous goals have been met as well as becoming a greater, stronger, and more competitive personal brand!

I will now leave you with 6.5 "Final Bites," which are the most important nuggets of information for you to remember. If you are feeling a bit overwhelmed or aren't sure where to focus your energies, let these 6.5 Final Bites be your guide. By themselves they will not allow you to bring Fresh PASSION into your life and career, but they will serve you well as general guideposts. Follow these 6.5 pieces of advice, and you will at least be headed in the direction of building a fresh, competitive brand, rather than suffering through the agonizing generic death that results when your brand is stale, out of date, and does not offer the substance or packaging necessary to stand out in the marketplace.

1. There is a reason that "Fresh" is the first word in Fresh PASSION. You must keep your attitude, outlook, skill set, reputation, network, and brand fresh at all times. In the Internet age, information and ideas are distributed, digested, and spat out at a pace that was never before imaginable. What is innovative and interesting today can literally be outdated and dull by tomorrow. So you must always stay fresh—never assume past success guarantees anything in the future, always take opportunities to develop new skills or contacts, keep up with the constantly changing needs of the marketplace and regularly evaluate how well your brand meets them.

    Furthermore, you must radiate freshness by dressing neatly and in fashion and displaying true confidence in yourself and your abilities. Otherwise, you may find yourself lumped in with the "day old" stale bakery products, selling for a dollar a dozen!

2. Success is impossible without setting a real, specific aspiration and remaining laser-focused on it. Remember, aim at nothing and you're guaranteed to hit it! And when I say aspiration, I don't mean something vague like "make a six-figure salary" or "start my own company." I mean something specifically tied to your unique skills, capabilities, interests, and passions that genuinely represents who you are and what you stand for.

    Your aspiration should also tie into your perfect day, which is how you would live your life if everything were exactly as you wanted it. Don't be afraid to set your aspiration extremely high.

Even if you only achieve 75 percent of it, three-quarters of a lofty aspiration is a lot more rewarding and fulfilling than three-quarters of a low aspiration! Remember, you should answer these three questions about your aspiration(s):

- Am I passionate about it?
- Do I have the skills to make it happen?
- Am I determined to make it happen?

3. To help you be prepared to demonstrate your brand value to any audience in any situation, you should have a set of processes and tools in place that will help you succeed in any job interview, client meeting, or other formal or informal situation where you may have the opportunity to promote your brand.

    By constantly reviewing your skills and experiences and determining exactly how you could leverage them to provide value to a potential employer, you can keep your arsenal fresh to keep up with the changing needs of employers, as well as your own changing needs. This arsenal is a weapon that will help you maintain the highest levels of internal and external competitiveness at all times.

4. Humans typically form a lasting impression of someone within the first three seconds they meet them. That means that by the time you walk through a door and shake someone's hand, they have essentially already decided how much they trust you, how much they like you, and whether they want to do business with you. You send out hundreds of signals about yourself, and people read those signals and react to them long before you've had a chance to say anything of substance.

    As mentioned in Step 1, it is important to dress neatly and stylishly and to radiate genuine confidence. But this alone will not guarantee a good three-second impression. After all, it is difficult to know how you may appear to somebody else, despite how well you think you come across! So ask trusted colleagues, friends, relatives, and your Branding Board to honestly assess your three-second impression and give constructive feedback. Like the old saying goes, "you never get a second chance to make a first impression."

5. You will undoubtedly encounter negativity throughout your career. It can come from rivals and competitors as well as from well-meaning friends, relatives, and colleagues who think they are "helping" you by dissuading you from following your aspirations. And the more success you achieve, the more negativity you will encounter. It is of paramount importance for you to omit this negativity from your life and your thoughts, but in a positive manner. Rather than seeking revenge on a backstabbing colleague, either win them over through your hard work and team approach or simply outshine them with your superior skills and brand so that their efforts at sabotage have no chance to succeed. You cannot control the thoughts and actions of negative people, but you can control how you respond to them.

6. You are a human being. Human beings are innately fallible. This means you will undoubtedly make mistakes on your journey toward achieving Fresh PASSION, building a successful brand, realizing your aspirations, and living your perfect day. You will not always follow the precepts of Fresh PASSION 100 percent of the time, nor will you always act in a positive manner that best suits the needs of your brand and career.

    When you stumble, don't panic. Most important, don't assume you've "screwed it all up" and there is no hope for recovering whatever brand equity you have lost. There is always hope, and unless you make a genuinely catastrophic mistake, you will be able to undo it with a little time and effort. I'm not asking you to be perfect, just the best you can be.

6.5 Remember to have a little fun! Success should be fun, and if you are working toward building a brand and achieving an aspiration that genuinely reflects who you are as a person, much of the work will be fun. But you still need to allow yourself a little time for rest, relaxation, and recuperation. Celebrate important milestones, like new jobs, promotions, or major client wins. Schedule the occasional agendaless day or agendaless week and allow yourself to unwind. Leave yourself time to pursue outside hobbies and interests, and understand that family, health, and spiritual needs come before anything else. You can't be fresh and passionate if you are a work-obsessed robot, so loosen up. Very few people have a perfect day that involves 24 hours of work!

About Michael D. Brown

Michael D. Brown developed a customer service process *(6.5 Fresh Steps to World-Class Customer Service)* that during the past 15 years has been credited with reengineering and enhancing the customer service strategy and experience for a number of small, mid-sized, and Fortune 500 companies, including Marriott, Macaroni Grill, U.S. Army, Wendy's, Omni Hotels, Houston Rockets, Capital One, Wells Fargo, Greater Houston Partnership, Jason's Deli, Amoco Oil Company, ARCO Oil Company, Murphy Oil USA—The Wal-Mart Project, British Petroleum, and a number of colleges and universities. Michael was ranked in the top 5 percent among high-performing leaders and coaches in leading Global Fortune 500 companies. He is a globally recognized authority on customer service leadership for developing this customer service strategy that delivers to the front line and three levels up in the user's organization. This work was later turned into the best-selling book *Fresh Customer Service—Treat the employee as #1 and the customer as #2 and you will get customers for life.*

Michael's success story is even more impressive considering his humble roots. Growing up as one of 10 siblings with a widowed mother in Holmes County, Mississippi, statistically among the poorest counties in the United States, Michael early on resolved to break the cycle of poverty and dead-end jobs that plagued so many of his friends, neighbors, and relatives. Starting at the age of nine with a job as a low-paid handyman and housecleaner for a verbally, mentally, and physically abusive boss, Michael quickly learned the importance of satisfying the customer and always doing the best possible job and having a brand of excellence, regardless of the circumstances.

He went from being supported by welfare to starting his own highly profitable candy-selling business (generating about $40 a day and quickly blossoming into a $300 to $400 a day business) in high school to support himself and the family, and then he worked his way through Jackson State University with a job as a cook at a fast-food restaurant, where he cut the average wait time at the drive-through window almost in half, achieved record sales, and received multiple raises within six months—but was not initially allowed to work directly with customers in the front of the house because of the "unwritten" rules. Despite this action, Michael continued to deliver greater results than all of his co-workers and stayed focused on delivering excellent results. After months of begging to work in the front of the restaurant, he was given a "trial shift," which turned into a night of customers raving about his superior customer service and leaving over a dozen positive comment cards.

After graduating, Michael, who holds a BBA in management and an MBA in global management from Jackson State, embarked on a highly successful executive career where he consistently boosted profits and employee morale at companies in the hotel, food and beverage, oil and gas, and retail industries. It is this unique perspective and know-how gleaned from his upbringing that makes Michael a sought after speaker and career and management consultant, and the leading authority on delivering fresh results.

With a track record of delivering double-digit top- and bottom-line growth to his clients, Michael is able to take a problem and look at it five to seven levels deep, allowing the delivery of strategies and solutions that are detailed yet simple and impactful while focusing on the overall strategies and sustainability of the achieved growth. He has a unique ability to break down the complex strategies and processes into a simple and executable strategy that can be delivered with passion and conviction by the front line at every step of the value chain.

Michael's expertise in revamping how companies provide world-class customer service and establish a market-leading brand has led him to assisting individuals in creating personal brands that allow them to achieve otherwise unattainable levels of personal and professional success. He is recognized for this best-in-class coaching strategy that yields consistent results.

Michael has motivated and helped thousands of entrepreneurs, military personnel, individuals, college students, graduates, and small-business owners move from a stage of generic mediocrity to an exciting place where they become successful personal brands that yield exponential personal economic and professional success. His signature work *Fresh PASSION: Get a Brand or Die a Generic* is the catalyst for helping individuals make the transformation to achieve world-class success.

Michael's ultimate message is this: Without a personal brand, you don't have a career—you only have a job. When you are a "generic" individual, there is only so far you can go in a given job, and it's only a matter of time before you're replaced. If you develop a dynamic personal brand, however, you differentiate yourself from your competitors and become a force to be reckoned with. Nothing will keep you from personal, economic, and professional success.

About Michael D. Brown's Brand Logo

We love brand ambassadors and we encourage them to spread the word about Fresh Results®. However, it's important that you communicate the essence of your logo, what it means, how to represent it, and how to treat it. You have to protect your personal brand. We actually have a brand identification guide that spells out the essence of our logo, how to represent it in print on the Web, how to put it together, etc.

My brand is delivering Fresh Results through and with people. The brand is represented by a Fresh Results emblem, consisting of a multicolor mint leaf. The leaves represent the results of good seeds (my proven and results-driven processes and solutions) that have been planted in good soil (the individuals, companies, organizations, military, etc., who are recipients of my good seeds) receiving proper nourishment and attention.

The four colors that represent freshness are dark green (left top leaf), light green (right top leaf), blue (left bottom leaf), and white (right bottom leaf). The leaves are symbolic of the fresh results I deliver as a speaker, coach, trainer, and author.

To see the full-color logo, please see the book flap. To see one of my complete business cards, please visit www.MyFreshBrand.com.

RECEIVE MY FREE eNEWSLETTER AND 52 FRESH PERSONAL BRANDING TIPS

I trust that you extracted value from this book. To continue receiving fresh and valuable information, please go to MyFreshBrand.com and sign up for the powerful eNewsletter and amazing 52 personal branding tips.

ORDERING INFORMATION

Fresh PASSION: Get a Brand or Die a Generic is available at www.MyFreshBrand.com, Amazon, Barnes & Noble, and other fine bookstores and online outlets. Please contact us for quantity discounts. The book is also available to the book trade and educators through all major wholesalers.

READY TO ENGAGE WITH A RESULTS-DRIVEN SPEAKER, COACH, AND TRAINER?

To book Michael for speaking and training engagements, please go to www.themichaeldbrown.com and submit a request form.